LORD SHOW ME YOUR PURPOSE

Teresa Walls

Lord Show Me Your Purpose
Copyright © 2018 by Teresa Walls

All rights reserved. No part of this publication may be reproduced, distributed, or transmitted in any form or by any means, including photocopying, recording, or other electronic or mechanical methods, without the prior written permission of the publisher or author, except in the case of brief quotations embodied in critical reviews and certain other noncommercial uses permitted by copyright law.

Although every precaution has been taken to verify the accuracy of the information contained herein, the author and publisher assume no responsibility for any errors or omissions. No liability is assumed for damages that may result from the use of information contained within.

Library of Congress Control Number: 2018965816
ISBN-13:   Paperback: 978-1-64398-106-2

Printed in the United States of America

LitFire LLC
1-800-511-9787
www.litfirepublishing.com
order@litfirepublishing.com

Contents

Listings of Books and Quotations Marked 1
    Lord Show Me Your Purpose

Acknowledgment 3

Forward 9

Introduction 11

Lord Show Us Your Purpose 19
    Esther 4:13-14

Spiritual Inheritance 23
    Galatians 4:1-19

Cut Covenant 27
    Genesis 15-17

The Importance of Prayer 31

Highest Form of Prayer (Synergy) 37
    (Matthews 18:18-19)

Seven Deadly Hindrances to Prayer 39

A Holy Fast 41
    Isaiah 58:1-12

Standing in the Gap 45
    Genesis 18:17

Count the Cost 49
    Luke 14:25-33

Don't Count God Out Jesus Is Able to Resurrect
This Dead Situation in Your Life 53
    St. John 11:1-44

The Comparison of This Generation.. 57
    Luke 21:32-33

Set Your House in Order.. 61
    2 Kings 20:1-2

Relinquishing the First Adam's Nature to Embrace
The Mysteries of The Kingdom of God... 65
    Ephesians 4:17-32

A Workmanship... 73
    Ephesians 2:10

The Goodness of God 77

Forgiveness God's Perfect Will 81
    Matthew 18:21-35

A Spirit of Obedience... 85
    Hebrews 5:8

Living A Life of Humility... 89
    1 Peter 5:5-6

The Love of God.. 93
    John 3:16

The Fruit of The Spirit 97
    Galatians 5:19-26

Walking in the Character of the Holy Spirit 101
    Galatians 3:2-3

THE GIFTS OF THE SPIRIT 105
    I Corinthians 12:1-11

God's Divine Unity 113
    Psalms 133, John 15:1-11, Acts 2:41-47,
    Acts 4:31, John 17:21-23

Afterword 117

Family Photos 121

Listings of Books and Quotations Marked

Lord Show Me Your Purpose

1.) The Knowledge Commentary (Old and New Testament) By John F. Walvood And Roy B. Zuck copyright © 1973, 1978, 1984, the International Bible Society. Use by permission of Zondervan Bible Publishers.
2.) World Harvest External Studies Program (Prayer God's Communication) By Rod Parsley copyrights © 2005. Printed by Results Publishing. Used by permission.
3.) 30 Days to Understand the Bible by Max Anders copyrights ©1988, 1994, 1998, and 2004, the International Bible Society. Use by permission of Zondervan Bible Publishers.
4.) The Every Day Life Bible (amp) Unless otherwise noted, all scripture in the Everyday life Bible is taken from The Amplified Bible and is used by permission of the Lockman Foundation and the Zondervan Corporation. Additional text copyright © 2006 by Joyce Meyer. Used by permission.
5.) The Power of Simple Prayer Copyright © 2007 by Joyce Meyer. Used by permission.
6.) Break Through Covenant Partner Devotional Bible (KJV) by Rod Parsley copyright ©2000 Published by Results Publishing. Used by permission.
7.) Walking in The Spirit copyright © reprinted 1990 by Gloria Copeland KCP Publications. Used by permission.

Acknowledgment

I give praise and dedicate this project to my Lord and Savior, Jesus Christ, for inspiring me to write this book. In addition, to my loving husband, Charles Walls, for a prophetic word to go ahead and write a page a day for all of his support expertise and encouragement. To Charles Walls Jr, for his encouragement everyday he loves his mother, I could never do any wrong as far as he's concern. To the Walls for Christ Family, thank you for being a support to the vision and for your genuine love. Thank you for all of my family: Tammy for being such a loving sister and a support to me. Eileen, Karen and Jeff, for being sensitive to the voice of God, and being a vital support to me. To Fred (Pop Pop) and Shirley (Mom) for treating me like your own. To my own parents Fred Jackson and Inez Thompson, who were always there for me. I dedicate this book to the both of them, and that it would remind me of what they placed in me through the Holy Spirit to always reach for goals in the Lord and the talents that they passed on.

Tell a Friend about Jesus

Tell a friend about Jesus,
how he touched your soul
Tell a friend about Jesus,
how he lifted you and made you whole

Tell a friend about Jesus,
house of prayer, how he led you there
Tell a friend how Jesus is teaching you about
his love, tenderness, and all he does.

Tell a friend about Jesus,
and how he makes you brand new
Show your friend in God's Word
what you learned and how you grew.

Tell a friend Jesus' kingdom is coming;
tell all of your friends do not delay
Tell them how Jesus died for them;
just say he will be here one day.

—Inez Thompson

My mom, Inez B. Thompson, was the greatest mom in all the world to me. There was nothing I could not share with her. She was the epitome of a loving mother. I first discovered the love of God through my mom. She always made me feel like I was the best thing that ever happened to her. I am sure she made my other siblings feel the same. We all thought we were her favorite. My mom has gone on to be with our heavenly Father, but she was my "she-ro" and always will be.

Fred R. Jackson was strong in demonstrating his gift of protection for us. We knew his qualities, and we respected them. Dad showed his love by what he did for us in holding us together, and I appreciate that in a father. Thank you, Lord for this special gift that you afforded me. Dad, your memories will always be in my heart. You have showed me that dads like you are rare and that they only come once in a lifetime.

Charles F. Walls Jr. is my hero. The one thing I love most about Charles Jr. is his spirit. He's always carefree, not worrying about a thing. He encourages me so much. In addition, I am enjoying having him in my life.

Forward

Teresa Walls approaches this subject of "Lord Show Me Your Purpose" with a sincere desire to impart to the reader pearls of wisdom, insight, and knowledge. What was refreshing was how we were captivated by her personal experiences and spiritual revelations. We were intrigued as we discovered how we experienced many of the same struggles and questions early in our own Christian life. In retrospect, many of us as babes in Christ have faced similar challenges as we began our journey to becoming a mature believer.

As a dedicated minister of the Gospel who walks in the gifts and as a woman of God who takes the call to intercession seriously, she has definitely developed a super-natural ability to recognize the ones who are crying out. You feel her deep desire to target the ones who need a divine encounter and manifestation of the true and living God. These are the ones who are in need of spiritual "road signs" to lead them to God's perfect will and plan.

Her passion to guide us as believers toward our purpose in Christ is evident in her transparent writings, examples, and expressions. There is no doubt in our minds that she will answer many questions for the new believer, will re-establish the faith of the mature Christian who knows their calling, and will inspire many to discover their true divine purpose in the Body of Christ.

Our Father wants us to truly be a magnet and a beacon to all. This book will give the believer the courage to choose the process of transformation in order to become an anointed servant of God. (Rom 12:1-2).

Jeff and Karen Woods
Fort Washington, Maryland, Elders

Introduction

Here I am the seventh offspring of nine siblings in my family. How could God have a purpose for me? There are too many of us, will He ever notice me? I would ask myself. I came from the wrong sides of the track, from a poor, dysfunctional family where there was no hope or prospects for anyone. My mother was a cosmetologist, and my dad was a special policeman in a common law-marriage where there was no foundation. I felt I didn't have an example, at the time, of how I would make it. In the mist of family arguments, partying, and crammed in a one-room apartment, there was very little room for getting to know who you were. I will never forget being so frustrated. I wanted so to make it in life, but all around me was negativity.

Even though I was not born again, I would pray all the time. I cried out, to God "Lord show me your purpose! Show me what you have for me!" In my environment it did not seem there was any hope. I would just cry myself to sleep to keep from thinking about my situation.

After so many years of going through such a depressed state, the bottom finally fell out. It was the best time and the worst time of my life. The worst time because my parents finally decided to go their own separate directions in life. In addition, the best time because for the first time in my life, I had made one of the most important decisions: to receive Jesus as my Lord and Savior. From that day forward my life had never been the same. It was the best decisions I have ever made. My parents were good loving people, they just did the best they could with what they had. They shelter us and gave us a decent life. They taught us moral integrity from their point of view. I love my parents and would not have traded them for any amount of money in the world. They took us to a point, and then God took over. Scripture says when father and mother forsake you, then the Lord will take you up (Psalms 27:10 KJV).

I came to a cross road in my life: to go my own way, or to go through a process and give birth to the life that Jesus Christ had shown me. It was a hard choice, because what God had shown me seem impossible. Moreover, from where I stood, I knew there was no way I could accomplish what God promised me on my own. When I began to allow the Lord to process me, He began to speak truths and secrets that made me believe that anything can be possible through Him. Therefore, I began to believe. No one could ever convince me that God's Word to me is not true. Then, after so many years of waiting, the Lord began to confirm to me through others, such as through the five-fold ministry gifts. They were telling me things that the Lord had told me in private that no other human knew. There's just no way that the things the Lord said could ever come to pass in my life through human effort. Therefore, I had to begin to trust the Lord to bring them to pass with my corporation.

There has to be agreement with the Lord for the purposes that He has for us to come to pass in our lives. God wants to do a miracle for us, but through us.

One of the reason's I decided to write about purpose: because everyone has one. God placed each of us here with a purpose in mind. In addition, the Lord has a zeal that everyone should know his or her destiny. Paul said that before the world began, God preordained and predestined us in the image of His dear Son (Romans.8:29). "Moreover, that God, being a partner in our labor, knowing that all things work together and are fitting into a plan for good to and for those who love God and are called according to His design and purpose" (Romans 8:28, amp). There are many devices and plans in a man's heart; nevertheless, the counsel of the Lord, that shall stand Proverbs (Proverbs19:21). The Amplified says, many plans are in a man's mind, but it is the Lord's purpose for him that will stand.

I once heard someone say, "if you want to get God to laugh, tell Him your plans for your life." It seems that we have our own plans for our life, but the Lord has a divine purpose, destiny and future predestine for you. Jeremiah says, "I know the plans I have for you!" (Jeremiah 29:11). The Lord was speaking to Israel in the mist of captivity, letting them know that he had a future to prosper them and not to harm them. Therefore, He had to allow them to go into bondage to the Babylonian king to get their attention. Have you ever had God to arrest you in your tracks? Well, that's what He did to Israel, only it cost them seventy years of captivity. It amazes me that when God brings up our future, we start to talk about our past, and all that we went through and all we have come from. And even the circumstances we find ourselves in. We began to tell the Lord how we can't do what He's called us to do, because we are so involved in so many things, or our plates are so full, we have no time, or I'm too young or too old for the purposes of God in our lives. In addition, we tell God that what we are doing would better suit and please Him rather than anything He could ever offer. We began to give God our excuses, and unwanted advice on how to run our lives. My parents use to tell me, "Unless you have at least thirty years of experience and a track record of what you're talking about, then you are not qualified to give any advice to anyone." That sent me away running with my tail between my legs.

Many are the plans that we have, but it is God's purpose's that will win out eventually. One thing I've learned about the will and plans of

God, is no matter how long we put off operating in them, we prolong God's perfect will, and we continue on down a path where we're just spinning wheels in a life of dissatisfaction. We will never be satisfied doing our own thing. We were created to do the will of God, not our own. You may even prosper for a while, but it will eventually give way to God's purpose. We have to choose to operate in God's perfect will. I heard someone say that the safest place to be on earth is in the center of God's will.

One thing that I know is that you are not an accident. He did not wait until we arrived here on earth and then say, "What am I going to do with this one?" No! God said that before I formed thee in the belly I knew thee, and before thou camest forth out of the womb I sanctified thee, and I ordained thee a prophet to the nations (Jeremiah. 1:5, KJV). Therefore, God was acquainted with you before you were born. That's why there are so many believers who don't know who they are, and don't know their identities. We struggle with our relationship with the Father, and we are insecure within ourselves because we don't know purpose. I can identify with those same insecurities, because until the Lord showed me who I was, I did not know and thought that I did. I wondered around aimlessly in my Christian walk, never really being able to identify in my relationship with Christ. Therefore, I took it for granted. I never got serious about my walk in Christ because I really did not know how. Moreover, I did not know what to ask of the Lord, even though the Lord knows what we need before we ask. Therefore, through difficult circumstances, the Lord caused me to "cry out." My cry was not for what I was going through, but it was a cry for what I needed. I was tired of wandering in the wilderness and I needed answers.

The Lord with His infinite knowledge began to reveal to me a glimpse of His purpose for my life, although I did not know how it would happen, or what I had to do or go through to bring it to fruition. Only God knows the end from the beginning. That's where our trust in God is.

It's been some years since the Lord showed me His will for my life. It's been unfolding in my life one step at a time. I believe it would be a life time of just seeing the total and full manifestation of all that God has in store for me and for those who love God and are called according to His purpose (Romans 8:28, KJV).

I have discovered by dealing with many in the Body of Christ that people have never really known their true selves. It's just like our DNA coils which is called chromosomes. Human cells have twenty-three pairs of chromosomes. Body organization begins and stems from the cell and progress systems. It's the same way each one of us stems from our very purpose in life. I believe that once we have tapped into our purpose then we discover who we truly are.

Purpose is the real reason that any of us exits. It's the only reason that we live. I believe that everything should stem from our purpose in life, the same way cells function. When cells are properly carrying out their functions, the tissues and organs work correctly also. So, when we tap into destiny, that's when life really begins for the believer. Health begins to spring forth. Prosperity comes forth to accommodate and support what you were place here to do. Because what God orders He's obligated to pay for.

Elijah realized that his season had changed for him, when the brook dried up and the raven stop coming to feed him; he knew there was another assignment in store for him. And the word of the Lord came unto him saying, "Arise get thee to Zarephath, which belong to Zidon, and dwell there: behold, I have commanded a widow woman there to sustain thee" (1 King 17:6-9). Our assignment can be long term or short term it doesn't matter, but our purpose remains the same. Elijah's assignment may have changed, his geographic location was in another place, but he was still the man of God, the prophet of God. Why do we think that things should never change in our lives— alternatively, that we can't flourish if things don't remain the same?

"Jesus is the same yesterday, today and forever," (Hebrews 13:8, KJV). Even though Jesus' ways and methods change, He remains the same. "For I am the Lord, I change not," (Malachi 3:6, KJV)

One thing I have notice about the Lord's character is that He's faithful. You can depend on the Lord to keep His word. He won't tell you something and not come through. "God is not a man that He should lie, neither the son of man that He should repent. Hath He said, Alternatively, hath He spoken, and shall He not make it good?" (Numbers 23;19, KJV). The Lord is consistent, He's constant in His character. He will never let you down. He is a Holy God, meaning He's different. He's different than any of those so-call gods that are made with wood and clay, that don't have eyes to see nor ears to hear and cannot speak. It is a blessing and a privilege to serve the "true and living God." He's a God that is in "touch with the feelings of our infirmities but was in all points tempted like as we are, yet without sin" (Hebrews 4:15, KJV). You can always place your trust in Him. Wherever He tells us to go, or whatever He tells us to do, we can be assured that Jesus will be there to see us through.

When we as the Body of Christ begin to obey the promptings of the Holy Spirit, I believe that order would began to flow throughout the Church. Moreover, we, as a Church Body would begin to line up with the Word and will of God, then we will see the Church, in its entirety, triumphant. "But the people that do know their God shall be strong and do exploits" (Daniel 11:32, KJV).

I heard my spiritual father say that "where the will of God is unknown, perfect faith cannot exist but where the will of God is known you let nothing turn you away." My prayer for the Body of Christ is that the Lord would open our eyes of understanding, that the eyes of our understanding would be enlightened, and that we would know what the will of the Lord is (Ephesians 1:17-19). In the mist of peril and trying times, even when people are stressed and preoccupied, people still desire to know the will of God for their lives. There are so many people doing things or are even dwelling in places where they are not satisfied or discontent. We, as a society struggle to know the deep things that lie in our hearts but are too busy to take the time to commune with ourselves. That's why we have such frustrated and stress-out people that we are dealing with from day to day. Don't get me wrong, there are people whom we come in contact with from time to time that are very much in touch with themselves.

One of the first steps in knowing who you are is coming into a personal relationship with the Lord Jesus Christ. Once you receive Jesus into your heart there's an experience that brings about a satisfaction that's unquenchable. You will never be the same again. "If any man be in Christ He's a new creature; old things are passed away, behold all thing are become new" (2 Corinthians 5:17, KJV). Once you begin to develop your relationship with the Lord, then you are on your way to finding out what the Lord has in store for you. One of the most precious experiences that you can have is when you are introduced to the ministry of the Holy Spirit. He is such a gentleman. He will woo you by His love. He will not speak of Himself but will bring up to you those things in which He hears, and He will bring all things to your remembrance (John 16:13, KJV). He will begin to comfort, lead and guide you unto all truths.

If you have not received Jesus into your heart, pray with me right now. Dear Jesus I'm a sinner, please forgive me of all my sin. I confess them now. Come into my heart Lord Jesus. Make me your child that I may live with you forever in eternity. Fill me with your precious Holy Spirit. In Jesus name, amen. If you have prayed that prayer, now you are born- again and are a part of the Body of Christ Hallelujah!

We serve an Awesome God who knows what we need before we ask Him. He will not leave you comfortless. Begin to read your Bible every day and get connect to a Bible based church continually.

Lord Show Us Your Purpose

Esther 4:13-14

Then Mordecai told them to return this answer to Esther, do not flatter yourself that you shall escape in the king's palace any more than all the other Jews. V14 For, if you keep silent at this time relief and deliverance shall arise for the Jews from elsewhere, but you and your father's house will perish. In addition, who knows but that you have come to the kingdom for such a time as this and for this very occasion Esther 4:13-14, paraphrased.

Many of us know the story of how Queen Esther became queen. Esther was born with the name Hadassah. Her name was changed to Esther (which mean hidden from) to hide her identity. She was a Jewess, who was placed in a position in which she could help the nation of Israel. Mordecai found out the plot against the Jews by the wicked Haman, a descendant of Agagite of six hundred years ago. Don't think that because Haman was a high-ranking Persian official that he could not be influenced by a "familiar spirit." We tolerate that spirit in our homes, at church, and at our jobs. If you go back into Haman's lineage, you can trace his ancestors all the way back to the Amalekites. Long before the time of King Saul, in the days of the wilderness wandering, Israel had been savagely attacked from the rear by the Amalekites, a deed the Lord had promised to avenge someday (Exodus 17:8-16). Saul disobeyed a command from the prophet Samuel to utterly destroy them. Saul refused to obey the prophet Samuel. Many years later, the Jews were faced with this same spirit to wipe the Jews out.

Moreover, Mordecai, Esther's uncle and foster parent, sent word to Esther saying, "Look here, miss sister thing. Don't think because you are the queen that you are exempt from perishing. Just because you are up there now, hiding behind those palace walls, don't think that the king won't find out that you are from the hood. In addition, who knows that you were put there for such an occasion as this."

Therefore, Queen Esther had a role to play. She had a purpose other than just being Queen. She was not positioned and put there to take up space in the palace, nor to impress all her homies. No, she was strategically place there to deliver a nation.

Now this is where the church comes into being. The Church was given birth by our Lord and Savior, Jesus Christ, to play a specific role in the earth realm. "To save much people alive" (Genesis 50:20b). "Jesus said upon this rock I will build my Church and the gates of hell shall not prevail against it." In addition, Jesus had another cause, "For this purpose the Son of God was manifested that He might destroy the works of the devil" (1st John 3:8). So here we have a two-fold mandate. In other words, the Church is here to get souls saved and to destroy the works of the devil. That's our mandate. Jesus did not save us to go to Church only. He did not save us to warm padded pews and hide behind four walls. We each have a purpose. That's the very reason we are here on this earth: to give God the Glory and to fulfill God's purpose and plan for our lives.

God has such a unique and original plan that no one else can fulfill it but you. God said, "I know the plans that I have for your life, says the Lord! Not to do you harm, but to give you hope in your final outcome (Jeremiah. 29:11, AMP). God says that, "Before you were in your mother's womb I knew you and ordain you" (Jeremiah 1:5, AMP). God has already predestined you. That means He already had plans for you when you were only a thought in His mind.

That's why we have a lot of professing Christians who struggle in their Christian walk. They don't know who they are. They struggle with God's perfect will for their lives. We would rather settle for His permissive and "acceptable" will (Romans.12:1-2, KJV). That's when He allows you to carry out your own plans for your life, and when you mess your life up and become desperate for God's will like the prodigal son that's when He steps in and presents His perfect plans that He had all alone for you. Do you think Esther did not have her own plans for her life? There was a risk in going before the king. Had not the king extended the scepter unto Esther, it could have meant her life. Yes, there will be risk in serving God. Yes, there will be risk in taking on God's assignment as oppose to what it is we would like to do for God.

Deborah, another person of the Word of God who made a difference, was a female judge. This was unheard of in that day and time. She refused to allow despair and injustice to take place around her was a prophetess and apostle of the Lord. She took on a role. "In the days of Shamgar, son of Anath, in the days of Jael, the roads were abandoned; travelers took to winding paths. Village life in Israel ceased, ceased until I, Deborah, arose, that I arose a Mother in Israel," (Judges 5:6-7 KJV). Deborah had enough on her plate. She did not have to do anything else. She was already a wife, probably a mother, and a Judge over the land tending to the affairs of those who came to her. However, something happened to her, she began to sense that there was another call on her. In addition, something stood up on the inside of her. She led an entire army alongside Barak to enter into battle to take back Israel, and the women Jael, dealt the final blow to Sisera. They were a team of warriors, two of whom were women, who went to battle to take back a nation.

Lord Show Me Your Purpose | 21

Moreover, we as women of God needs to get a resolve in our spirit and take back our nation, take back our children from the streets. Get angry at the devil instead of your church family. For instance, say, "Devil, I have had enough!" How many of you are sick and tired of being sick and tired? Then we need to take a stand against injustice that we see all around us. Moreover, begin to take our rightful place in Christ, to exercise our authority on the enemy. We tolerate too much stuff in the Body of Christ that cause us to be put in bondage and chains because we won't stand in the authority that was given to us, thinking we don't have any control over our situation. Stop letting the devil take residence in your home, your church your job, over your children finances. Tell the devil enough is enough! Jesus has given us all power to tread on the devil. Stand up and take authority. Whatever we tolerate won't change. Come on. Whatever we keep putting up with won't change. God wants us to stand up and be the Church, that He's calling for in this last day. Will the real Church stand up! Stop being that Laodicean church, that lukewarm Church that's neither cold or hot (Revelation.3:14-16). Come on, the Lord is trying to wake us up, to wake the sleeping giant from her slumber. "It's time for us to wake from our slumber, for our salvation is nearer than when we first believed" (Roman. 13:11, KJV).

Spiritual Inheritance

Galatians 4:1-19

"We are those who are heirs of salvation, so as long as the inheritor [heir is a child or immature] he does not differ from a slave, although he is the rightful owner of it all" (Galatians. 4:1-2, NIV).

What is a slave? A slave is a servant, someone that is told what to do. You have to tell them to come in and go out; they don't think for themselves. Although, a son is heir, he's immature to handle his estate. So, therefore he's under guardians, administrators or trustees until the time appointed by the Father. That's where spiritual come in. This is where the process of God begins. This is where we come in to sonship, is when we begin to allow God to process us. A many of us do not ever come into a relationship with the Father, therefore, they can never enter into becoming spiritual sons and daughters.

Formerly, we in our state of spiritual immaturity, when we were like children, we were like slaves, whether under the basic principles of the world or under the law; whether we were in the world under bondage or religious bondage. God sent His son to redeem or emancipate us from the bondage in His appointed time. To redeem us under the law that we may receive the adoption of sons; (Galatians 4:3,4,5). And because God sent His son to set us free, it is essential for us to come into our purpose and allow the Holy Spirit to begin to process us for our inheritance. Alternatively, we crucify the Lord of glory a fresh.

Paul is saying but because you really are His son, God has sent the Holy Spirit of His son in our heart, crying Abba Father; (Galatians. 4:6). You can't call God the Father Abba accept by the Holy Spirit. Therefore, you are no longer a slave (bondservant) but a son; and if a son, then it follows that you are an heir "by the aid of God, through Christ; (Galatians. 4:7). In order to become a son or a daughter to any human authority you have to have proper relationship or intimacy with God the Father through Jesus.

Prior to conversion the Galatians, in their ignorance of the one true God were in bondage to false gods such as Zeus and Hermes. However, a great change had taken place and they came to know the True God then began to turn back; (Galatians.4:8-9). See for some of us we are in a good time, and a vulnerable time. We have allowed hopelessness, and weariness to creep in. And some of us even had thoughts of giving up altogether. But, "Be not weary in well doing, for in due season you will reap if you faint not" (Galatians 6:9b). For instance, for those of us who are being delivered from bondage of religion, did you know that we have to fight the good fight of faith? In addition, sometimes, we may get weary. (Second Corinthians 4:8-10, KJV) says, "We are trouble on every side, yet not distressed; we are perplexed, but not in despair, persecuted, but not forsaken; cast down, but not destroyed. Always bearing about in the body the dying of the Lord Jesus, that the life also of Jesus might be made manifest in our body."

Here Paul travailed over these Galatians as if he were giving birth; until Christ was born in them; (Galatians 4:19). Travailing is a deep intercession (standing in the gap) for another. It is an intense suffering in the inner man. However, that's what it will take, until we are one with the (will and purpose of God for our life). Until Christ desires becomes our desires. Until His affections become ours. Until we die to our life and deny ourselves, then will we find life. However, there are those who still have not completely sold out to God. We are still not committed. We still want to hold on to our old life and holding our own selves up to receiving our inheritance.

"Now brethren, I commend you to God, and to the word of His grace, which is able to build you up, and give you an inheritance among all them which are sanctified" (Acts 20:32).

Cut Covenant

Genesis 15-17

Since the beginning of time, God established covenant and imparted anointing with His choices of servants. Throughout the Bible and recorded history, great men and women have shared in covenant of faith to impose change in their generation.

We live in a time when a person's word means absolutely nothing. Marriages are dissolved daily with no regard to vows of "until death do us part," and our courts are flooded with lawsuits. However it has not always been this way. In Biblical times, a covenant, sealed in blood, was a promise of enduring responsibility never entered into lightly and never disregarded. This is the kind of relationship we have with God. The entire Bible is a legal covenant signed in Jesus' Blood. The word testament means "covenant or agreement." In the Old Testament or (covenant) there are 5 books of the Law which is called the Torah or Pentateuch; 12 books of history, 5 books of poetry, 5 major prophets and 12 minor prophets. In the New Testament (covenant) the first five books are Historical, the next thirteen books are Pauline Epistles and the next nine books are General Epistles. All established upon better promises.

What exactly is a covenant? A covenant is an agreement between two parties. It is usually made for three specific reasons- protection, business and love. Let's look at (Genesis 15:1-12 and 18).

We see here in Genesis 15 that God is making a covenant with Abram base on the promise he made with him in Genesis 12 where he told him, that He would make him "father of many nations." Now what made God choose Abram out of all the people in Israel? Why did God make a promise to Abram instead of his father Terah? Glad you ask. One of the reason God didn't choose his father was because he worship pagan gods. However, Abram paid a tithe to Melchizedek, then the Lord formally made a covenant with Abram, thereby confirming the promise given to Him (Genesis 12:2-3). God made a promise to Abram, but in order for God to bring it to pass Abram had to show faith towards the promise by initiating his belief in what was promised. In other words, Abram, had to prove (trust) God. The Bible said Abram staggered not against the promise of God through unbelief but was strong in faith giving glory to God (Roman 4:20). Moreover, it was accounted to him for righteousness. Abram had to do his part by connecting himself to the covenant.

You see, you can have a promise by God, but unless you connect by faith to show God that you are in agreement with the covenant then, that promise would lie dormant. Once we do our part by acting in faith or agreeing with the covenant then God's does the rest by keeping the promise. For when God made promise to Abraham because He could swear by no greater, He swore by Himself, saying, "Surely blessing I will bless thee, and multiplying I will multiply thee" (Hebrews 6:13-14). And so, after he had patiently endured, he obtained the promise. The reason why some of us are unstable in our walk with God is that we need to cut covenant, because you have many of folks who are not committed to anything, let alone to Jesus. Let something happen to shake your world. A lot of us have told Jesus "Later- for- you dude. See ya wouldn't wanta- be- ya!" See some of us are just having an affair, a rendezvous with the savior. As long as the blessing are trickling down we are satisfied— when Jesus is making you aware that He has inheritance for you. See this thing is not about you, it's bigger than you! Jesus is not after your money. He wants to establish a 'legacy" with you. God wants to make purpose and promises come to pass in your life that He has establish before the foundation of the world. It's about receiving your inheritance to pass down to your seed, your "children's children." Let's look at Genesis. 15:2-5.

God wants to cut covenant so you can pass it on to your posterity. When God spoke to me in 1989 about purpose, it stabilized my entire life. Many of times, we think we know who we are in Christ but we really don't know. God spoke one word (Jeremiah 1:5) and it change my life. Now, I don't know what it all entails. But it was enough to line my life up with His Word. When Abraham cut covenant everything in his house cut covenant; they were circumcised in the flesh. When God established covenant with Abraham's house, He will cause everything in your household to line up with His will. "For I know him, that he will command his children and his household after him, and they shall keep the way of the Lord, to do justice and Judgement; that the Lord may bring upon Abraham that which he hath spoken of him," (Genesis 18:19). You don't have to pull teeth and manipulate to get people to do what God is saying to them, just cut covenant with Him. You will begin to see everything go in the direction God intended for your life.

Not only did Abraham cut covenant, Moses, made a covenant when God sought to kill him, to try to do what God commission before doing what He commanded. Joshua did make a covenant for the city of Jericho. David cut covenant at the threshing floor to stop a plague. Moreover, Jesus did to become the mediator of the new testament or covenant which was established upon better promises. Jesus our mediator wants to established us upon better promises because of the blood covenant He made when He gave His life and placed His blood upon the mercy seat to redeem us from a life of sin.

Lord Show Me Your Purpose | 29

The Importance of Prayer

Why is it so important to pray? Well, whom do you think the devil is more reluctant to use, the spiritually minded man or the carnal minded man? Yes, you are right. He's unwilling to use the spiritually minded man because he/she guards their hearts with prayer. That's why it is important to pray and stay connected in prayer and in the Word. You're more alert to the devises of the enemy and can advert them by staying in tune to the Holy Spirit than you would if you're not sensitive or in prayer.

The scripture says to watch and pray lest you enter into temptation, to be alert as well as pray. We have to keep our spiritual ears in tune with God. In addition, keep the lines of communications open with God at all times. You may say, "How can I pray at all times with uninterrupted prayer?" Well, you can keep a posture of prayer and fellowship of prayer without concentration. It is fellowship and communing. We do it every day, on a social level. Well it's no difference when we are fellowshipping with God. Prayer is very intimate. Moreover, you become sensitive when God is calling us to pray. Your antennas are on alert when God is on you to pray. Scriptures says, "Men ought always to pray and not faint" (Luke 18:1).

We may have the mechanics of prayer. We know how to pray eloquently. We may even know how to quote scripture and know how to make it sound just right. However, James 5 says, "The effectual fervent prayer of the righteous availeth much." For example, if your prayers have not changed you, don't expect it to change your circumstances, don't expect it to change your children, your spouse— although prayer have the capability to change anything. However, it first has to change you. The reason I believe we in the twenty-first century Church don't see much of our prayers answered is because we are not having a lifestyle of prayer operating in our lives. We want the "quick fix" thing going on with God, and He's not buying it, because the Lord knows when you are sincere in prayer. When we pray in secret He rewards us openly (Matthew 6:6). In addition, many of us are praying just to get something from God and we really haven't made a real commitment to prayer. We really have not submitted ourselves to God's will for our lives. You know how I know? It's because, it amazes me when something comes up that we really want to do and it interferes with God's will. I notice our choices. That's how I know we're not submitted. One of the reasons I believe the Lord is focusing us on the importance of prayer is because, prayer is essential to our Christian walk. Prayer solidifies (to make solid, to change one from unstable to grounded) in our faith in God. It's just like a car with a motor. Try taking the motor out and see how far it will run. Prayer is vital, its necessary. It's our communication with God. Prayer is one of our weapons of warfare; you can't go into battle without it. But we treat prayer so casually, as if to pick it up only when we need it. Prayer is our only way of petitioning God. Prayer is our source to communicate with God. I want to begin in the book of 2 Chronicles 7:14-15.

Second Chronicles. 7:14-15: is a charge to the church, for I believe if we the church, was on our knees praying, society would be in a better place. Moral Clarity would not be in a declining state. In addition, not to say that we don't have people that God has raised up to intercede. Nevertheless, I believe that God has called others as well. Stop saying that you are not called to intercede. Everyone in the Body of Christ is called to intercede. "Many are called but few are chosen to intercede" (Matthew 20:16). That responsibility lies with the church. The scripture says, "For unto us a child is born, unto us a son is given, and the government shall be upon His shoulders. And He shall be called wonderful, counselor, the mighty God the everlasting father the prince of peace," (Isaiah 9:6). In other words, because the government rest on the shoulders of Jesus, the responsibility lies with the church. If my people... Jesus is not talking about the world. He is talking to those who are called by "his name" would humble themselves and pray. We are in a war. The problem is trying to get us to realize it. Oh, we are praying when the enemy is wailing on our heads. However, let all be going well for us. God doesn't hear from us.

Why did Jesus speak this parable of the unjust Judge? Because Men ought always to pray and not to faint. Jesus teaches on the parable to show us persistence in prayer and not to give up. Our problem is at the first sign of trouble, we back off from prayer, and He does not hear from some of us until a week a two later. This unjust judge would not hear the widow's case, but because of her persistence— not because she had the best defense lawyers, but because of her continual worrying, she drove the judge nuts. He decided to give in to her. Moreover, how much more will God through our persistence in prayer, grant you your petition and quickly, though He bear long with us (Luke 18:1-8).

The reason for this parable about the publican and the Pharisee is that one cannot trust in himself for righteousness and view others with contempt. We know how we do. Why can't so and so speak in tongues "like" I do? The only thing you have to do is just open your mouth and just speak. We have to be careful not to become haughty with a gift that was given like the Pharisee. Praise God if you can pray for an hour, but don't view others with contempt if everyone is not like you. The publican realized all he could do is just throw himself on God's mercy seat, saying, "Lord just have mercy on me a sinner," (Luke 18:9-14).

God's purpose is on our Knees:

When Jesus was in the garden of Gethsemane, Jesus tells the disciples to pray lest they enter into temptation. Only prayer can keep us during temptation. That's why it is so important to pray and not wait until temptation is upon us before we begin to pray. Layup prayer like the one Hezekiah did so when trouble comes, you're not overcome by it. I believe if the disciples had prayer in the garden like Jesus ask they would not have denied Jesus; they would have endured long with Jesus not counting their lives dear to them. Moreover, we see here in Matthews 26:40 Jesus ask, "Could not you watch with me one hour?" I believe that the Lord is not saying we have to pray an hour necessarily, but I believe if we practice an hour daily, if we practice His presence, we would begin to see some breakthroughs in our lives. Some of us probably have spent less than thirty minutes in prayer, start where you are. Nevertheless, I see this as a model for prayer time (Luke 22:39-46).

First Thessalonians 5:17: "Pray without ceasing," meaning continual prayer in order to have a posture of fellowship with God as much as possible in the midst of daily routine in which concentration is frequently broken. Not a prayer that prevails without interruption or uninterrupted prayer. Perseveringly, meaning to continue effort in spite of difficulties— stead-fastness: persist steadfastly. You can't just pick up prayer and expect and answer from God. I believe when God sees the sincerity of your persistence that's when he answers.

The conclusion is clear: "Therefore confess your sins to each other and pray for each other" (James 5:16). A mutual concern for one another is the way to combat discouragement and downfall.

The cure is in personal confession and prayerful concern. The healing (that you may be healed) is not just bodily healing but healing of the soul as well, (Matthew 13:15; Hebrews 12:13; 1 Peter 2:24.) It is powerful and effective ... prayer of a righteous person that brings the needed cure from God.

The world's greatest untapped resource is "prayer." People have not tapped into it. They would rather find some other way of getting their needs met. They would go through all kinds of circumstances just to avoid laboring in Prayer. Hosea 4:6 says "My people are destroyed for a lack of knowledge." The only difference between you and defeat, and you and someone that's in victory is "knowledge." That person takes the same knowledge that you both received and "exercised it."

Prayer can give you the knowledge and wisdom you need:

You have to devote time to prayer; you can't give God this drive by prayer and keep giving Him the excuse, that I just don't have the time to pray. Then baby, you don't have time for yourself. Because when you devote time with God you are taking the time for yourself. When Jesus got ready to select His disciples He went in prayer all night long just to be able to hear from God. Some things take time to turn around in prayer. You can't give God five minutes and expect Him to do the miraculous, although He's capable.

We have a command to pray. First Samuel 12:23 says, "Moreover as for me, God forbid that I should sin against the Lord in ceasing to pray for you."

We have a command to pray. "Whosoever commit sin transgresses also the law, for sin is the transgression of the law." (1st John 3:4). "Therefore, to him that knows to do well, and do it not, to him it is sin." (James 4:17). Sin is breaking the Law. Neglect is sin. The sin of omission carries the same weight in penalty. The command of God is neither optional nor flexible.

Prayerlessness is sin. When we neglect the very thing that holds our structure together then we are in violation to the one we are praying to. However, God can't tolerate sin. We cut our own selves from our source. We are left without a covering which is prayer. Moreover, sin separates us from God.

"But thanks be to God for giving us the victory. God has given us access to Him, through His loving son Christ Jesus!" (1st Corinthians 15:57).

Highest Form of Prayer (Synergy)

(Matthews 18:18-19)

The highest form of prayer is the prayer of agreement. When we agree in prayer, touching anything that we shall ask, it shall be done for them of my Father which is in heaven. Agreeing in prayer is not just two or more persons coming together just to get what they want from God. On the other hand, we will end up with a situation such as Nimrod in (Genesis 11:2-6) where they synergistically put their minds together and came up with a project that left God out of the equation. God Himself declared that a people whose hearts and minds were in agreement could not be restrained from doing anything they imagined. Unity and agreement is a key factor of the effectiveness of any local agencies or local church. The total effect is greater than the sum of their effects when acting independently. Agreeing in prayer is the sum total of unity in the faith. When our hearts and minds are coordinated with purpose and vision that we are following for the greater good, it's not to get what "we" want." That's why a lot of times we could be praying in agreement with someone who really don't agree with us and our prays are null and void; there's no unity and no agreement.

The prayer of agreement is only effective when those who come into agreement in prayer are living in agreement in our natural, everyday lives. Living in agreement does not mean we cannot have our own opinions about anything, but it does mean that there is harmony, mutual respect, and honor in our relationships. It means there is an absence of the things that cause division and strife- like selfishness, anger, resentment, jealously, bitterness, or comparison. Living in agreement is like being on the same ball team- everyone works together, supports and encourages each other, believes each other, and trusts each other as they all pursue the same goal and share the victory. The same that should be in marriage relationships. It's hard to maintain unity and agreement when both parties agree outwardly but secretly the other parties heart is somewhere else.

Jesus says in Matthew 18: 19-20 "Again I tell you, if two of you on earth (harmonize together, make symphony together about whatever (anything and everything) they may ask, it will come to pass and be done for them by My Father in heaven. For wherever two or three are gathered (drawn together as My followers) in (into) My name, there I am in the mist of them." God is also with us as individuals, but our power increases as we come together in unity and agreement. The Bible says, that one can put one thousand to flight and two can run off ten thousand (Deuteronomy 32:30). God's blessing rest on unity and His presence is with those who agree in His name.

When you have been praying about something and don't seem to be making any progress, you may need to get somebody to pray in agreement with you. That kind of unity is a powerful spiritual dynamic, and according to Psalms 133, it is good and it commands God's blessings upon you. When two or more people come into agreement, Jesus Himself promises to be with them, and His presence exerts more power than we can even imagine in our lives and in our circumstances.

Seven Deadly Hindrances to Prayer

1.) Prayerlessness- Prayerlessness is sin. When we refuse to pray, God can- not change or work on our behalf if we do not give Him anything to work with.
2.) Sin- Sin is as sure way to cause God not to hear you. Sin separates from God.
3.) Praying outside the will of God. Praying outside the will of God can keep us from getting our prayers answered.
4.) Unforgiveness- Unforgiveness is the number one reason prayers are not answered.
5.) Rebellion- A person who intentionally disobeys God and authority will never prosper in God.
6.) Pride- God resists the proud but gives grace to the humble. A proud person can easily block their prayers from being answered by not walking in humility (Prov.16:15; Prov. 21:4).
7.) Lack of Gratitude- A lack of gratitude indicates that something is wrong in a person's heart, and a thankful heart is necessary for answered prayer.
8.) Worry- Another reason why people's prayers are not answered, because after we pray then we worry (Ephesians 6:18).
9.) Not caring for people in need. If we want our prayers to be answered we need to be compassionate to the poor (Proverbs 21:13).

10.) Failure to focus- Prayers are not answered because we fail to focus when we pray and we are not diligent to keep our hearts connected to heaven. (Proverbs 11:27).
11.) Negative Confession- When we allow doubt and unbelief to set in our heart then we began to speak negatively, we hinder our prayers.
12.) Doubt and unbelief- Are opposites of faith and will keep our prayers from being answered.
13.) Praying with wrong motives- James 4:2: "We do not have because you do not ask but do ask and fail to receive because you ask with wrong purposes and evil, and selfish motives."
14.) Lack of boldness- Praying with fear and unreservedly. We feel that our prayers won't be answered because our hearts are already filled with fear, we haven't built trust in God in our walk. And we pray as if we don't deserve what it is that we are asking for. We have no confidence/ we can come boldly to the throne room of God because we have been made to be the righteousness of God. And we can pray with total confidence and pray un- ashamedly knowing that he loves us, hears us, and will answer our prayers in the best possible way.

A Holy Fast

Isaiah 58:1-12

In my many years of devotion and consecration to the Lord, I have discovered that you can't do one without the other, "fasting and prayer." I have been on every kind of fast there is: a water fast, juice fast, vegetable fast. I have fasted watching T.V. and fasted to lose weight. I came to the realization that I didn't have a clue to what I was doing. Until I ask the Lord to help me in this area of my life. I truly wanted to know how to live a fasted life style. I went to the book of Isaiah 58 by the direction of the Holy Spirit and read that if I wanted to learn to fast then I must fast "a holy fast." What is a holy fast? A holy fast, I believe, is when we live a fasted lifestyle, as we began to do introspection on those things that are in our hearts that vexed the Holy Spirit.

God use heralds or proclaimers; bearer of messages, forerunners to remind the people of their sin and transgression (Isaiah 58:1). He told them to "cry loud and spare not; lift up thy voice like a trumpet" (Isaiah 58:2). I began to read Isaiah 58. I told the Lord, "I can't go around telling folk about their sins and transgression, and what does this have to do with me?" Bear with me now, there's more to this conversation.

He said, Outwardly I seemed eager to want to know Him and for God to be near me. This was an outward show, He told me.

My concern in Isaiah 58:3a was of the people who voiced their concern that they were in difficulty though they seemed to be doing what the law required. They fasted and humbled themselves, but they feared that God had not seen it or noticed. Apparently, they thought that by going through the "motions" of religion (without any inward reality of faith) they would be blessed.

The response of the Lord: Lord responded by pointing out that He was more interested in our obedience than our rituals (Isaiah 58:3b-14). Unfortunately, we, like many people, had confused rituals with relationship, outward acts with true obedience.

Our fasts did not alter or change our poor relationship with others. We are disregarding other peoples' needs by exploiting others, by quarreling and fighting. Therefore, our prayers would not be heard, for our kind of fasting was not what the Lord accepted. Our hearts, not just our heads, needed to bow before the Lord (Isaiah 58:3b-5).

Fasting was to encourage a person to respond positively to God's commands. In the Old Testament, only one fast was commanded: "the annual day of atonement" (Leviticus.16:29). Nowadays we have folk announcing their fast. Matthews 6:1-2 says, "When you do your alms (fasting and praying etc) do not sound a trumpet; do not do your alms before men to be seen of them, otherwise you have your reward of your father in heaven." When we do fast, it's not about what we will give up or how long we fasted or prayed. It's not boasting of how spiritual we are. Rather, our fasting and praying is to break the demonic off us so that we are positioned the more to hear from God.

A man had bought his son to the disciples to cast a demon out but could not, Jesus said, "Bring him to me." Jesus cast the devil out. Moreover, the disciples were baffle, saying, "Why could not we cast him out?" Jesus said, this kind comes but by "fasting and praying." In addition, some of us are like Satan casting out Satan. A house divided against itself can't stand. You can't have the demonic inside of you, then calling yourself casting the devil out. The demonic has to first be destroyed off you; then will you have the power to cast him out. That's why we are living in situation where there's a lot of demonic activity going on around us, and we feel we don't have the power to do anything about it. However, we have authority through the shed blood of Jesus.

When we began to fast and pray the spiritual world knows that we are beginning to position ourselves to launch an all-out attack against the forces of darkness. You are telling the devil enough is enough. I'm taking my family back. I'm taking my health, wealth, and my territory back from the enemy. Everything the devil has stolen I'm taking it back. I'm recovering it all! You're not going to be like the seven sons of Sceva in the book of Acts, who went up to the demonic saying, "I adjure you in the name that Paul knows, the demonic said, Jesus I know, Paul I know, but who are you?" In addition, they were sent butt naked running for their lives, (Acts 19:13-16). No, the spirit world is going to know your name. Every time you set your feet to the floor in the morning, they will know that you are on the warpath against the forces of darkness. You and the name of Jesus will be a force to reckoned with.

Standing in the Gap

Genesis 18:17

Standing in the gap is pretty much an awkward position to be in. It can be a very uncomfortable place to be in because you pretty much are standing as a representative of Jesus. You're standing as a sign or a plumb line for God, that someone else could know that there is a God somewhere. Moreover, we are indescribable. You are the go-between. It's not "popular" in the church. Many intercessors find themselves in this position. God is raising up a people to "stand in the gap!"

Moreover, "I sought for a man among them, that should make up the hedge, and stand in the gap before me for the land, that I should destroy it: but I found none" (Ezekiel 22:30). No one seeks God to make up the hedge. Everyone seeks for prestige— in the church, the more common positions. Abraham stood in the gap, he stood in the gap on behalf of Sodom and Gomorrah. God said, "Shall I hide from Abraham that thing which I do" (Genesis 18:17). And the Lord said, "Because the cry of Sodom and Gomorrah is great, and because their sin is very grievous; I will go down and see whether they have done altogether according to the cry of it, which is come unto me; and if not, I will know. But Abraham stood yet before the Lord. And Abraham drew near, and said, wilt thou also destroy the righteous with the wicked?" (Genesis 18:20-23). Here Abraham stood before the Lord and standing in the gap on behalf of Sodom and Gomorrah that God would not destroy, if at all He could find at least one righteous man. God is still looking for those who would stand in the gap today, to stand for His purpose against all odds. I have heard a few people say how God has them at a church, or how he sent them there just to intercede. And that was their only purpose. What an unpopular position to be in some would say, but noble. How many people do we hear of saying that they are standing in the gap for others? Very few. We may hear, well I'm a minister, or I'm a pastor or musician, or a soloist. However, none would ever confess that God just uses them to intercede. You don't hear this preached from the pulpit. You may ask yourself, well what does standing in the gap means? I'm glad you ask the question. Standing in the gap is a mediator, those who go between and brings about peace or agreement. To settle disputes, or differences. God sent Jesus to be our mediator, our go- between. Jesus stood in the gap on our behalf as a mediator between God and man. He was sent to redeem man back to God.

"And for this cause he is the mediator of the new testament, that by means of death, for the redemption of the transgressions that were under the first testament, they which are called might receive the promise of eternal inheritance" (Hebrews 9:15). Christ is the mediator of that covenant, and the inheritance is available to those who are called since the death of the mediator has freed them from all guilt derived from the sins committed under the First Covenant. Jesus our mediator; "obtained a more excellent ministry, by how much also he is the mediator or the (go between) of a better covenant, which was established upon better promises" (Hebrews 8:6).

There's a responsibility that come along with standing in the gap. Remember earlier on I spoke of this position not being a popular one, but noble. You see in order to stand in the gap for someone, something has to die in order for something to live.

The Hebrew writer talks about the death of the mediator. That by means of the death, for the redemption of the transgressions. In order to stand in the gap, you are in some way treated as a "scape-goat." A scape-goat in ancient times was an animal who was chosen to bear the sins of the entire community and to be punished by death or banishment (Leviticus 16:21). In other words, this animal was instead wrongfully blamed and punished for the mistakes and failures of others. In the Old Testament, they would use, bullock for sin offering, lambs without blemish for thanksgiving offering and sheep and of the goat for a burnt offering. While Standing in the gap you may encounter some of these experiences for someone else. Your whole purpose is to die (to self) so that someone else may reap the benefits of salvation. What a noble position to be in. You may say, "I never want to stand in the gap for anyone." Well then, your witness is in vain. In other words, if you can't die for what you believe then what good is your living? "For where a testament is, there must also of necessity be the death of the testator. For a testament is of force after men are dead. Otherwise, it is of no strength at all while the testator lives" (Hebrews 9:16-17). A person who stands in the gap for someone else can't claim anything for its own. All that he does, all of his sacrificing, and all of the death process that he experiences in his members, are for someone else. So, in other words, all that you may encounter for standing in the gap is for someone else, not for yourself. The mysteries of an intercessor are unheard of. No one talks about it; no one wants to do it.

I believe there are those in the Body of Christ who assumes this role, because no one seeks God for it. I can recall on a number of occasions how my husband and I found ourselves assuming this role by the aid of the Holy Spirit, because of our compassion for churches without a pastor. All that a church goes through during the transition is phenomenal. However, the aid of the Holy Spirit, could raise you up to assume a role to stand in the gap. Some may call it during the interim period. However, even doing those times of interim, God never leaves us alone. God is still looking for someone to stand in the gap. Would you consider the call by the Holy Spirit for a mighty work? God desires to use you, and together, we can do exploits for the Lord. Assume the role of "Standing in the Gap" for the Lord today.

Count the Cost

Luke 14:25-33

Here, we see in the fourteenth chapter of the book of Luke is showing us another side of the Father if we look back at the sixteenth verse where Jesus is given this parable about a great feast that took place and how everything was now made ready. In addition, the good man of the house began to beckon many. Moreover, he began to send his servants out, but the story went on to say that many began to make "excuses." Many are called but few are chosen. In addition, that's what we are seeing happening in the Church today there are too many of us making excuses. Jesus goes on in verse 26 and says, "If any man come to me, and hate not his father, and mother, and wife, and children, and brethren, and sisters, yea, and his own life also, he cannot be my disciple." Jesus makes a profound statement here, but what Jesus is conveying here is, "In order to be my follower you have to forsake all."

And here they say that literally hating your own family is violating the law, but Jesus is not getting anyone to break the law; but He's stressing one's loyalty and love for Him should be a higher priority.

See, what Jesus is dealing with His Church is, He is tired of competing with us and our emotions, our feeling, and our wants. It's not that He does not want us to have anything; it's that we have to start putting our loyalty in the right place.

The second difficult qualification Jesus stressed was that one must carry his own cross and follow Jesus. Back When the Roman Empire would crucify a criminal, the victim was often forced to carry his own cross part the way to the crucifixion site. This signified that the Roman Empire was right and the criminal was wrong. Therefore, when Jesus entails His followers to carry their cross, saying that He is right and that they would follow even until death. I believe the Lord is allowing us to pause for a moment and to hear what the Spirit is saying to the church. He is saying, "Count the Cost." I believe this is an end time message for whosoever today as well as to the Church, because there are too many of us making excuses to the Father. We want certain things from God, but we are not willing to make any sacrifices for Him. Oh, we will come to Church and hear the word of God, but when he speaks to us and give us instructions to do something that may inconvenience us in any way, we are ready to give up and throw in the towel. We don't want to go the distance, we don't want to go the extra mile. There are those in the Body of Christ who are not willing to give up anything, or do something that may help someone else, let alone themselves to advance the Kingdom. Timeout for being a spectator on the sidelines, watching and pointing fingers of whomever is not getting it right. Well, at least they had the guts to get in the fight. See, some of us wants something for nothing. We want what we want, but without cost. Let me tell you spiritually it won't work. Jesus says, "Work out your own salvation with fear and trembling." That means He's not carrying us but for so long. He expects us to mature in Him and to give birth to our own faith. He expects us to carry our cross and follow Him.

Here, Jesus taught that discipleship must include planning and sacrificing, that before building he should be sure he will be able to pay the full cost of the project (Luke 14:28). Jesus followers must also be sure they are willing to pay the full price of discipleship.

Moreover, this is where most Christians get stuck; they settle right here. They start out alright, but when they get going and begin to see the sacrifices and the long hours. And that you have to be patient with unruly people, and not kick everyone to the curb— and love and be kind. Then they began to drift away. They began to draw back. Jesus said, "those who put their hands to the plow and looking back, is not fit for the kingdom of God" (Luke 9:62). Moreover, we are not where we should be in the Body of Christ. Somebody ask you to do something, and you told them no, because you thought you wasn't qualified. Each time we make excuses we tell God no, and we regress a little further away. See we want ministry but we are not counting the cost. I hear a lot of folk say I'm call to preach, because they see a man or a woman behind the podium. However, they fail to see all the studying that goes into standing behind the podium as well as living the life and the long hours spent in prayer to hear from God. Because you can't get up there with your opinions or talking about your problems. You got to have a word from God!

The second illustration concerns a king who went out to battle. The king should be willing to sacrifice a desired victory if he senses he is unable to win. This principle of sacrifice is also important in the realm of discipleship; one must be willing to give up everything for Jesus. Let's face it. We haven't given up everything. We think we have. "Oh, I have made Jesus Lord over everything." No, we haven't. If the Holy Spirit was to bring up something that we were holding on to, we would deny it. Let Him ask you to give up something that you desire the most for Him. Count the cost!

Don't Count God Out
Jesus Is Able to Resurrect This Dead
Situation in Your Life

St. John 11:1-44

This climactic miracle of raising Lazarus from the dead was Jesus' public evidence of the truth of His great claim, that "I am the Resurrection and the Life." Death is the great horror which sin has produced (Rom. 5:12, James 1:15). For when lust hath conceived, it brings forth sin: and sin when it's finished brings forth death. Physical death is the divine object lesson of what sin does in the spiritual realm. As physical death ends life and separates people, so spiritual death is the separation of people from God and the loss of life, which is in God. Jesus has come so that people may live full lives. "For I have come that you might have life and that more abundantly," (John 10:10). Rejecting Jesus means that one will not see life and that his final destiny is the second death: the lake of fire.

This Lazarus is mentioned in the New Testament only in this chapter and in chapter 12. Bethany is on the east side of the Mount of Olives. Another Bethany is in Perca. Luke added some information on the two sisters Mary and Martha. This Mary was the same one who later poured perfume on the Lord and wiped His feet with her hair. However, the sisters assumed, because of the Lord's ability and His love for Lazarus, that He would immediately respond to their word about Lazarus' illness and come. There may be a situation in your life that is ready to die or have already died but hold on "Don't count God Out" don't think that because God loves you, that He won't delay His coming. He may not come when you want Him but He's always on time. Some of you may have experienced a midnight crisis in your life. Your dream has died, there's nothing humanly possible that you can do. This is a job for Jesus. Jesus said, "Do not count me out. I am the resurrection and the life. Though it (your dream) is dead yet shall it live."

Jesus did not come immediately. Nevertheless, His delay was not from a lack of love for Lazarus. He waited until the right moment in the Father's plan. You see, Lazarus was dead for four days, according to the scriptures. Jesus delayed His coming for two more days. See, this sickness was not unto death. What are you talking about preacher? Lazarus was dead, there looked like no way that he could ever live again. Yes, but this sickness was not unto death, but for the Glory of God. There are times in your life, when you are faced with a dead situation. Your promise from God is dead, your money has run out, sickness in your body and you can't get well. Moreover, the only thing you want to see is Jesus. This is a job for Jesus.

Habakkuk said, "Write the vision and make it plain, though it tarry wait on it. It will surely come" (Habakkuk 2:2-3). See, many times when we try to manipulate things to bring wicked devices to pass, we do it for our own glorification. We want to tell folks, "Look at what I done." Moreover, we leave God out of the process. However, this thing is not unto death. Therefore, I am going to raise it up that God might get the glory. Come on here, somebody. Jesus said, "I'm going to do it so you can't get the credit. Therefore, you won't be arrogant and say, "If it wasn't for me this thing would not have happened." It was not your prayers and fasting that did it. It was not done on the arms of flesh, but for the Glory of God. Martha told Jesus, "Lord, if thou had been here my brother would not have died. Moreover, I know that even now, that whatsoever you ask the Father He will give it to you. Jesus said, "Thou brother shall rise again." Martha said, "I know that, Lord, in the resurrection. Jesus said, "I am the resurrection and the life: he that believes in me, though he were dead yet shall he live, and whosoever lives and believes in me shall never die." In other words, Jesus said, "don't count me out." I know that your situation is deader than a door- nail. However, before you pack your bags, before you throw in the towel, before you throw up both hands, and decide to give up, don't count me out. For "I am that I am." I am the only one that can raise this thing back to life. I am the only one that can turn it around; I am the only one that can bring you the victory. "I am the resurrection and the life." The same spirit that called Lazarus from the tomb is that same spirit that raised Jesus from the grave — it will be the same spirit who can resurrect that dead situation in your life. Don't count God out. He is the only one that can bring life out of death. "O death, where is thy sting? O grave, where is thy victory. The sting of death is sin; and the strength of sin is the law. But thanks be to God, which gives us the victory through Jesus Christ our Lord!" (2nd Corinthians 15:55-57).

The Comparison of This Generation

Luke 21:32-33

"This generation shall not pass away until all be fulfilled," (Luke 21:32-33).

It amazes me how we, as the Church, are so involved with issues that don't have anything to do with "the great commission" of Jesus. Matthew tells us that Jesus said, "Go ye therefore, and teach all nations, baptizing them in the name of the Father, and of the Son, and of the Holy Ghost," (Matthews 28:19). I believe that once we get consumed with the mission of dying, men and women—and let's not forget our children, the next generation—then we will stop sitting around and get on about the business of Jesus Christ.

We are always looking for the next person to take up the slack in the Church as we sit on the side line waiting for a sign from God as to whether He is truly calling us to go and deliver somebody from the pits of hell. What's wrong with this generation? The Lord said, Wherefore, shall I liken this generation? (Matthews 11:16-19). Jesus is saying, "Whom can I compare this generation to?" He said, we are like children sitting in the market place, we have danced and mourned and you have not responded. Therefore, if that generation rejected the ministry of Jesus and John, Jesus is saying this generation is doing the same. We have sat back in this generation, and handed over our schools to murder and crime, we have murdered 125,000 innocent babies a day to abortions and counting. We are raising a generation that arose and does not know God. We are looking and seeking a sign from God or for something to happen or move us in the direction that God wants us to go in. Jesus said, that the Kingdom doesn't come with observation (Luke 17:20). In other words, if you are looking for a sign to come before you obey God then we are going to miss the "purpose and plan of God."

Jesus said, "This generation seeks after a sign. Moreover, "there shall no sign be given it but the sign of Jonah" (Luke 11:29). What did Jesus mean by this statement? What does Jonah signify in this era? A sign represented a confirming miracle. The crowds were not willing to believe Jesus except Jesus did some type of miracle. However, Jesus said, Jonah will be your sign. For instance, Jonah was a sign to the people of Nineveh. When they saw Jonah come up from the belly of that great fish, the people where convinced and repented. Moreover, when the prophet spoke, they obey. Jesus said, "How is it possible that when the sky turned red that it is fair weather and when the clouds move in then you know that it's going to rain? How is it that we can discern natural things but we can't discern the sign of the times we are in? (Luke 12:54-56). We ought to be sensitive to what's going on right now just like the sons of Issachar who knew the times. I can recall a time in my walk with the Lord of being passive and laid back, from walking in carnality, not knowing the principles of the Lord. I believe there are a lot of Christians who don't know any better, who are walking in carnality, and passivity and don't know it, because they don't have a close enough relationship with the Lord. There are those who don't desire enough of a "deeper walk," they just remain in a place that's superficial, just enough to get by.

We in the Church need to be sensitive to interpreting the things of the Spirit. We are hearing God. He is offering us the Kingdom. But we are not properly responding to the prompting of the Holy Spirit. We desire to be convinced before we obey the Lord. What areas of your life the Holy Spirit need you to quickly obey Him in?

Set Your House in Order

2 Kings 20:1-2

To set your house in order I believe is a mandate for those of us in the Body of Christ who may not know our purpose and destiny and the direction in which the Lord is leading us into.

Here, if you notice after Hezekiah's ordeal with the king of Assyrians, and God defeating the armies of King Sennacherib's army on behalf of king Hezekiah, the prophet Isaiah came to the king Hezekiah with a word: "Thus saith the Lord, "Set Your House in Order" for you shall die and not live!" King Hezekiah wept bitterly before God to grant him his life back to him. If you read on the Lord did grant king Hezekiah his request and added fifth- teen years to his life. Praise God that worked to Hezekiah's favor. I believe there's a "Clarion Call" to the Church at large, to "set our house in order, to get right with God." Moreover, that our priorities will line up with His will. We have many folks who are oblivious to the will of God for their lives; they're just Churchgoers. However, the Lord is requiring a commitment (deeper level) from those of us who claims they know Him, who desires to effect nations. God is preparing us to go into all the world and preach His gospel to all nations. Now, your world may be starting right in your own house, or in your community but that's His commission for our lives.

Isaiah says, "set your house in order for you shall die and not live". It seems like a kind of harsh and doom and gloom declaration. It's almost a final blow to Hezekiah. What is Isaiah saying here? I believe God is talking about purpose. If we don't find our purpose in life, we're like a dead man walking. We are existing without direction, living without meaning. We are as good as dead when there's no purpose. We are without hope. No vision, for without vision the people perish. Without hope there's no future. Many of God's children are living, but they are dead, there's no meaning to their lives, there's no direction. So, God is saying, "I want order!"

Here we see in the book of Revelations 3:2 Jesus speaking to the Church of Sardis, saying "Be watchful and strengthen those things which remain, that are ready to die: for I have not found thy works perfect before God." We the Church think that we are somewhere with God that we really are not; (1 Corinthians 10:12). He said, "Strengthen those things that are ready to die, for I have not found thy works perfect before God" (Revelation 3:2). Here we see God is warning the Church to set things right before Him. Set our house in order. Nourish those things. What things? Those things that are about to die. First, we, as the Church don't have an intimate relationship with Jesus. We have many Church goers who go to Church religiously. And then after church we put God back on the shelf until the next time we need Him. So, it's no wonder we as the Church can't obey God because we don't know Him. There are saints who are complacent with their walk with Christ and don't know what it means to "seek the Lord." We don't read our Bibles; we just go to Church because that's the thing to do, and we don't go any further. We want a fling with Jesus when He is looking for a marriage relationship with you. Moreover, "It shall be in that day," says the Lord, "that you will call me Ishi [my husband], and you shall no more call me Baali [my Master]," (Hosea 2:16).

Jesus wants a committed relationship with us so that we will experience dimensions in Him. When we talk about "new dimensions," I am merely speaking about new levels in the Spirit. We cannot just rest on our experience of salvation and settle there. Acts 1:8 says, "And you shall receive power after that the Holy Ghost is come upon you. In addition, you shall be witnesses unto me both in Jerusalem, and in all Judea, and in Samaria, and into the uttermost parts of the world." Some of us in the Church are afraid to receive the power of the Holy Ghost; we need that power to be endued (equipped) from on high, so that God can move us from a dead state in Christ. We are frustrated with our walk in Christ. It's because we are at a crossroad, and we need to go to the next level in Him. We need the Holy Ghost with power in order to be "witness" in the earth and to be able to live. Without it, we are carrying on the work of the Lord in our own strength and ability. God does not need our ability but our availability, where we may find ourselves operating outside of the will of God. Only the Holy Spirit can do a work in us and give us insight and the power to be effective to bring about results in another's life or in our own. There are those who may never go to church with us, but we can be an example before them. They can see the power of the Holy Ghost residing and resident on the inside of us being a living viable witness before family and peers in demonstration of what we claim to believe every day. We don't have to preach to people as we so desire to do. We can be a silent witness living the life style of a Christian before those around us and allowing the Holy Spirit to do the drawing.

My prayer is that we would allow the Lord and the power of the Holy Spirit to come into our hearts and bring in order, structure and the Holy Ghost power into our hearts, our lives, communities, and our churches. Moreover, He can do it, if we stop trying to.

Stop and say this prayer with me; "Dear Lord, thank you for drawing me to the cross. Forgive me of my sin. I'm a sinner in need of a Savior. Come into my heart and save me and abide with me forever. Be Lord over my life. Fill me with your Holy Ghost power that I will be a witness in the earth for you. In Jesus' name! Amen."

Relinquishing the First Adam's Nature to Embrace The Mysteries of The Kingdom of God

Ephesians 4:17-32

What am I saying here to relinquish the first Adam's nature? To get rid of the old man nature to secure the new man on the inside means to die to self- absorption and allow God's Spirit to have free reign in your life. The Bible calls it "to mortify the deeds of your flesh." What is the flesh? The flesh comprises of our mind, will and emotions, in which we need to starve out, and stop allowing them to have dominion over our spirit. And that really take a step of faith because you are actually changing your mind to doing things in a way that is unfamiliar to you, in order to begin to do things God's way. Moreover, we have many Christians who are still living a base, impure, carnal, mediocre, ordinary life. Someone who does not want to live right or wrong (double-minded), a person with an average life style, someone who don't want to make a difference, you're just straddling the fence; you' re not hot or cold. You have one foot in and one foot out— a unstable, wavering type of Christian. You get my point. In addition, the point is, that you're afraid to let go of your base life, because you're afraid that you have to give up something that is very dear to you. Moreover, you think that you are letting go of something. However, the truth of the matter is God has a life that far outweighs and over exceeds the base life that we want. God wants to give you an "abundant life." Christians are afraid of that. They are afraid that they have to give up their pet sins that we nurture every day. One of our pet sins is "self."

Do you know, we have been rebuking the wrong enemy for years? We have been rebuking the devil and his imps for decades. The real problem is, catering to our flesh (carnal nature). This is where Jesus has problems with the Church. See, nobody talks about dealing with the flesh, dealing with self. You see we like sermons that will not ruffle our feathers. We want sermons that will tickle our ears. We want to talk about things that will appease our flesh, that's going to make me feel good on the inside. We want stories and fables, that would nurture our pet sins. In the last days, people will not be able to endure sound doctrine (2 Timothy 4:3). The moment Jesus began to do surgery on this old flesh of ours, we want to get mad at the preacher. However, how can you hear without a preach? Jesus wants to sever us from our pet sins. He wants to do surgery. Will you let him. Okay, let's begin with the book of Ephesians fourth chapter we are going to do a survey on righteous living. Starting with verse 17.

Paul is speaking, to the Ephesians to walk no more as the Gentiles do, in the futility of their thinking. In other words, walking as we use to, when we were in the world; being darkened in their understanding and separated (alienated) from the life of God because of the ignorance that is in them due to the hardening of their hearts. In addition, that is what happens when we harden our hearts to God. We become unwilling to follow in his ways and we become insensitive. The scripture says, having lost all sensitivity (verse 19). Because of the lack of sensitivity, these Gentiles gave themselves over or abandoned themselves to sensuality, lust, licentiousness, debauchery, excess, a life style of impurity. Their purpose was to practice every kind of impurity with a continual lust for more. Indulging in self-gratification without regards for others.

This is a horrible picture of sinful people's selfish and perverted ways. This is dealing with our flesh. This is what God wants to do surgery on, the part He wants to do away with. This is what we have to give up: self-gratification, self-indulgence. Moreover, we, as Christians, can't have it both ways, there is no "demilitarize zone."

Well, that is talking about our old nature, our old-man. In verse 20-32, Paul gives an illustration on a righteous life, on holy living. Let's look at verse 20. Paul says, "You did not come to know Christ that way. Surely, you heard of him in accordance with the truth, you were taught the truth, that is in Jesus. You were taught with regard to your former way of life, to put off your old self, which is being corrupted by its deceitful desires; to be made new in the attitudes of your minds and to put on the new self, created to be like God in true righteous and holiness." Here, we see Paul is not speaking to unbelievers, he's speaking to those of us who have been washed in the blood of Jesus, those who profess the name of Christ.

These Christians were still living the way they use to. There was no change of heart. They had not gone beyond them receiving the Lord Jesus in their heart. In addition, many of us think that's all there is to salvation. We stop there, but Jesus says, "Work out your own salvation with fear and trembling." In other words, your salvation goes way beyond you receiving Jesus; that's just the beginning stage. Our minds are no longer darkened, our lives are no longer alienated from God, our hearts should no longer be hardened or impure. Christ should be the center of our lives. Christ teachings should be based on the truth because He is the truth. You know we, as Christians, have a way of twisting Scripture to make them fit our situation, but the Word of God is based on the truth. The content of the believers' learning should be based on two-fold. 1. A believer has put off the old self, which is being corrupted by its deceitful desires. Self-centered lust is deceitful because they promise joy but fail to provide it. 2. The believer has put on the new self, which has been created to be like God in true righteousness and holiness, which is based on truth.

We have many Christians going through persecution in the church. However, unbelievers are not persecuting them. Think about it. A lot of our opposition is coming from within. What I mean by that is we try to live a righteous life without first getting our hearts right with God. As a result, we come up against persecution from other saints, right in the church, when our greatest enemy is ourselves. The enemy lives within.

"Out of the abundance of the heart flows the issues of life," (Proverbs 4:23). Jesus said: "It is not the washing of the hands and these other rituals that we do that makes us clean. It is not what goes into the mouth that makes us unclean, but the things that comes out of the mouth comes from the heart, and these make a man unclean, for out of the heart proceed evil thoughts, murders, adulteries, fornications, thefts, false witness, blasphemies. These are the things which defile a man: but to eat with unwashed hands defiles not a man (Matthews 15:1-20).

Hear what the Spirit is saying. Our problems are heart issues, that we don't care to talk about; issues that the leaders in the Church are afraid to deal with. Issues with pride, arrogance, self-centeredness, lying, cheating unforgiveness which are but a few. Issues, that are going on right in the Church. And we sweep them under the rugs in the closet in our secret places so no one can know about them. Nevertheless, everything that is covered, God will bring to light. However, these are heart issues, they start as pet sins and then they manifest and become full-blown strong-holds which are difficult to get rid of. They started in the heart. That's the old nature, the Adamic nature, in which God is telling us we need not walk in any longer.

Here, Paul is admonishing us to put on the new man, to embrace the newness of life.

If any man be in Christ he's a new creation, old things are passed away, and behold all things have become new (2 Corinthians 5:17). Paul is not talking about our physical body. When we became Born

Again, it did nothing for our physical body. Instead our spirit was illuminated and quickened by His Spirit.

One of the issues Paul is admonishing us to put away is lying. Having put away falsehood, believers are to tell the truth (Ephesians 4:25). I can't stress that enough. Lord deliver me from lying saints. Always putting on a front. Can't be honest, with you, never mind with someone else. As if they have something to hide. Look, I'm not trying to get in your business, just because I ask you "how are you doing?" Then they begin to shift on you. They tell you they are going to do something for you. You don't even hear back from them "lying saint." We ought to tell the truth, put away lying with each other, keep your word, stop making promises or vows you can't keep.

Paul admonishes us to "Be angry, but sin not. Don't allow the sun to go down upon your wrath" (Ephesians 4:26). In other words, Paul is saying while we may have a right to be angry against sin, we have no right to take it to another level and sin. Some of us use our anger as a right to sin. Well, look at what so and so did to me! They really hurt me! God is saying forgive, don't let the sun go down upon your wrath. Don't keep dragging things on. Forgive, and move on. Suppose Jesus did that to us when we sort forgiveness. We would be up a creek. Paul says, "Neither give place to the devil" (Ephesians 4:27). You know the enemy love to take something minor and make a mountain out of it. Pastor Durham use to tell us "don't major in the minors." In addition, if we let him he would get into our little spats and the enemy would use one against the other. Then we are wrestling against each other instead of against the wiles of the devil. Paul said, "Let him that stole steal no more but rather let him labor, working with his hands the thing which is good, that he may have to give to him that needs" (Ephesians 4:28).

Ephesians 4:29 says, let no corrupt communication proceed out of your mouth, but that, which is good to the use of edifying, that it may minister grace unto the hearers." We, as Christians, are so hungry to be worldly, we have gotten to the point we are trying to imitate our children, instead of us trying to be an example to them. Paul said let no corrupt communication proceed out of your mouth." But that will encourage and build up. Stop tearing each other up with words, assassinating others' characters. Ephesians 4:30 "And grieve not the Holy Spirit of God, whereby you are sealed unto the day of Redemption." Do you know that we have many unhappy Christians in the Church today? Why? Because they are grieved inside. When you grieve the Holy Spirit, you make yourselves unhappy. You hurt yourselves when you don't allow the Holy Spirit to have full reign in your life. When you don't permit the Holy Spirit to have complete reign or dominion in you, therefore we make the Holy Spirit sad (GNV). He doesn't just want a part of you, He wants all of you. He wants to be Lord of your life, your first love. Because you are sealed until He comes back for you. So, there's no need to keep fighting against His Spirit living on the inside of you, you are actually making yourself miserable. Ephesians 4:31-32. Six vices that need to be discarded:

1.) Rage—an outburst of anger
2.) Bitterness— settled feelings of anger
3.) Brawling— shouting or clamor
4.) Slander— malice
5.) Ill will
6.) Wickedness— plotting and planning revenged.

In addition, put on being kind, compassionate, forgiving, being gracious, to each other as Christ have been forgiving to us.

Let's look at 1 Peter 1:14-16, Peter says, "As obedient children, not to fashioning yourselves according to the former lust in your ignorance." In other words, don't conform yourselves to the evil desires that governed you in your former ignorance when you did not know the requirements of the gospel. However, as the one who called you is holy, you yourselves also be holy in all your conduct and manner of living. For it is written, "Be ye holy, for I am holy." And we know to be holy requires being separate from the world. To be different. Here we see, in the book of Leviticus 11:44-45, the Lord instructing Moses to sanctify the children of Israel. As God's people were to distinguish between clean and unclean animals, so God had distinguished between them and other nations. Because He is our Lord and our God and that He is holy, therefore we are to be holy. Being holy is not something that we are not capable of being. It's a commandment from God because he has given us the ability to be. It's a state of being. Our original place in God. Be ye holy!

A Workmanship

Ephesians 2:10

"For we are his workmanship, created in Christ Jesus unto good works, which God hath before ordained that we should walk in them," (Ephesians 2:10).

"The Lord will perfect that which concerns me; Your mercy and loving kindness, O Lord, endure forever. Forsake not the works of your own hands," (Psalms 138:8).

"Let patience have her perfect work, that ye may be perfect and entire wanting nothing," (James 1:4).

"The God of all grace, who hath called us unto his eternal glory by Christ Jesus, after that ye have suffered a while make you perfect, establish, strengthen, settle you," (1Peter 5:10).

"Being confident of this very thing, that he which hath begun a good work in you will perform, complete, perfect it until the day of Jesus Christ," (Philippians 1:6).

All of these scriptures have one thing in common: that God will do a work or perform a complete work in us until the day He returns. So, there's no getting around it. A lot of us wants to graduate without going through grade school. However, in order to get to the next level, you have to pass the grade where you are.

That word perfect is the Greek word for complete. Which means God want to complete the work He has begun in us. In addition, the reason why a lot of us are walking around incomplete is because we don't allow God who is the potter to shape us and mold us into His image, (Jeremiah 18:1-6). He said completely, whole entire, lacking nothing. That means when God gets through with us we can graduate to the next grade level. Many times, we think we are ready. Moreover, we do this for God and do that. Saying, "Well God, I did this," and yet done that, trying to win God's approval. Only by the Holy Spirit doing the work on the inside will we ever be complete. Not by what we do superficially. Moreover, that's why we have many of folks in the church trying to work themselves silly trying to please God and it's not working. They are in everything— on every committee, on every program burning ourselves out, for to hear, God say, "I didn't tell you to do any of those things." However, the work God desires to do in us is an inner work. "For by grace are ye saved through faith; and that not of yourselves: it is the gift of God: not of works, lest any man should boast. For we are His workmanship, created in Christ Jesus unto good works, which God hath before ordained that we should walk in them," (Ephesians 2:8-10). God knows when we are complete.

He told Isaiah, "Speak comfortably to her, that her warfare is accomplished [complete], that her iniquity is pardoned," (Isaiah 40:1). See I believe that there's a releasing that takes place in the Spirit, that when you are ready, that thing that God has promise you would just show up. That's how you know. We don't have to make it happen it will just show up. Because promotions don't come from the east nor the west nor from the south, (Psalms 75:6).

Jesus went down to Jordan to be baptized by John. When he went down, the Scriptures said that the heavens opened and a voice as the sound of thunder spoke: "this is my beloved son in whom I am well pleased" (Matthews 3:17). Now what did Jesus do that God was pleased? Remember the voice did not say "well done." Jesus had not done anything, but came to fulfill all righteousness. He had not healed the sick nor raised the dead at this point. First, Jesus had positioned himself as a son. He submitted himself to John who was the spiritual authority. Then, second, Jesus recognized who he was and began to tap into his sonship. For the first time, he began to move into his destiny. He discovered what the will of God was for him. Jesus had not done one miracle at that time. He just allowed the Father to complete a work in him, and that's what pleased the Father. "It's not by works of righteousness that we have done, but according to his mercy he saved us by the washing of regeneration and the renewing of the Holy Ghost" (Titus 3:5).

Now that we are complete in Him, now that we have been perfected and promoted to another level, there's a completely new realm, and new responsibilities that comes along with operating on a new level. You know how it is when you graduate from high school and you go on to college. Your last years of high school prepped you for college. And you can't operate the same way you did when you were in high school. Well that's the same way it is when we graduate to another level in the Spirit. You basically have to learn to walk all over again. We get all excited about promotion. Then when we get there, we think we have arrived, and we kick back while the devil is waiting to sift you as wheat. Somebody said, "Where there are new levels there are new devils." We are relaxing, thinking we made it. That's how we do. You know how it is. We get that promotion on the job we have been praying for. We get there the next day "late." We begin to take longer lunch breaks, thinking I've arrive. No, what it took to get where you are, that's what it will take to keep your promotion. We, as humans, have a tendency to forget who gave us promotion in the first place. That's why God has to "process us." That's why He has to do a work in us to perfect us so we can handle our promotion; it's called "character." In addition, we ask, "Why is it taking so long, Lord?" I believe when we ask God for His best and the perfect will of God, that's when He began to do a lasting work in us, so we will be not ashamed and bring Him Glory! Amen.

The Goodness of God

How many of you know that God is a good God? We serve a good God. David says in the Psalms 100, "For the Lord is good and His mercy is ever lasting." "Then he said, "Oh taste and see that the Lord is good" (Psalms 34:8). Therefore, we see that God's character is good. His very nature is good. James says, "Let no man say when he is tempted, I am tempted of God: for God cannot be tempted with evil, neither tempt he any man. "Ironically, it is funny how we blame God for everything bad that happens to us. "For every good and perfect gift is from above and comes down from the Father of lights. With whom is no variableness, neither shadow of turning" (James 1:17).

Now let's look more closely at Exodus 33:18. Here, we see throughout this book Moses and the children of Israel had experienced God's goodness firsthand. Moses began to plead with God and stand in the gap for the children of Israel after they had erected a golden Idol before God and said, "This is what bought us out of bondage." Moses remember God's goodness at the burning bush. Moses had seen God's goodness when he went before Pharaoh to let God's people go. Moses witness God's goodness when he saw God demonstrate ten plagues upon the Egyptians. Moses saw when God delivered the children of Israel through the red sea on dry ground and they came forth on eagle's wings. He even remembered talking to God, face to face. Have you ever been so desperate for something? Moses was desperate for the goodness of God. He pleaded, "show me your glory." For instance, Moses desire to see a manifestation of God's goodness again. After all, God's anger was kindled against the children of Israel's rebellion. God said, thou shall have no other god before him. Three thousand souls fell as result. Moses repented because the goodness of God leads us to repentance.

Now, let's look at how we can cultivate one of the nine fruit of the spirit called goodness in our lives.

John 15:1 says, "I am the true vine, and my Father is the husbandman. Every branch in me that bears not fruit."

Notice, Jesus is talking about someone who is "in Him." They are saved, but they are not bearing fruit. What will our heavenly Father do to those branches?

"He taketh away: and every branch that bears fruit, He purges it, that it may bring forth more fruit" (v.2). The word purge signifies the cutting away of falsity, excess and pretense. (For the church, if we had the falsity, excess and pretense cut away from our lives, there would not be much left.) How do we bear this fruit? Verses 3– 5 tells us:

"Now are you clean through the word which I have spoken unto you. Abide in me, and I in you, as the branch cannot bear fruit of itself, except I abide in the vine; no more can you, except you abide in me. I am the vine, you are the branches: He that abides in me, and I in him, the same brings forth much fruit: for without me you can do nothing."

So, there you have it. Abide in Him and you will bear fruit. This brings God glory when He sees fruit bearing in us.

Now let look more closely to Exodus 33:18. Here, we see that the children of Israel had experienced God's goodness first hand; God had delivered His people from bondage. Then they turned around and got amnesia. Just that quick, they had forgotten the goodness of God. Moreover, how God bought them out on eagle's wings. God's goodness was so powerful that He open up the red sea and they walk across on dry land. However, because of Israel's rebellion and offering up idols before God, God's anger was kindled against the children of Israel. In addition, three thousand souls fell that day. God's anger was so kindled that He told Moses that He would not go up with them. Again, Moses stood in the gap. Moses pleaded with God and said, show me your glory. God's Glory is a manifestation of God's goodness. Therefore, God hid Moses in the cleft, and he saw God's goodness pass by. Moses repented on their behalf because the goodness of the Lord leads us to repentance. The goodness of God will change your life and turn you up side down, right side up. It will change your whole outlook on things even your circumstances. The goodness of God will give you a new perspective on life. You will never be the same again. Begin to get desperate for the goodness of God. Some of us feel guilty, because we think we do not deserve anything good to happen to us. However, God wants to show you His goodness just as much as you want it. Something good is going to happen to you today! Chineke Idinma! God is Good!

Forgiveness God's Perfect Will

Matthew 18:21-35

We can choose to operate in God's perfect will or his permissive will. God leaves the choice up to us. We can operate in God's best or we could choose to go our own way. It's up to us. In addition, the reason for that is, God is not going to stand there and twist your arm and make you do things the God kind of way. I always hear Christians say, Living for God is hard." No, "the way of the transgressor is hard" (Proverbs 13:15). Anyone living without God is hard. We know that living the God kind of way requires a higher standard of living that we need to adhere to. In addition, we also know in order to live for God in His perfect will that we have to depend on God. We cannot live the requirements, ordinances, and precepts of God without depending on God. You see, God Knows that. He knows that forgiving someone after they have wronged you over and over again would take the power and the anointing of God to get you through. Why? Because Jesus knows that offences will come. No matter what you do to get around falling out with another individual, the enemy knows just how to bring opposition in your life. The thief cometh, even though God is for us, the enemy will throw everything and the kitchen sink your way.

"Forgiveness is a gift from God, under the foundational stone repentance," (Hebrews 6:1-2). Repentance prepares and qualifies us to receive God's forgiveness and pardons.

God knows that forgiveness plays and important role in our relationships, because sin separates, unforgiveness severs communication, it hinders prayers answered. Unforgiveness can hinder God's presence and His very source of supply in your life. Many times, people try to receive miracles, healing, and prosperity from God, but they still want to continue to live with the sin of unforgiveness in their lives. Then wonder why they don't receive anything from God. It's because of unforgiveness. The scripture says, "And when you stand praying, forgive if ye have aught against any: that your Father also which is in heaven may forgive you your trespasses" (Mark 11:25). Jesus did not ask you how bad they hurt you. He did not ask for every nitty-gritty detail of the way they said something to you. On the other hand, how they are messing around on you, or they left you standing holding the bag. Jesus said "Forgive." I know that messes with our theology. We can't figure Jesus out. Nevertheless, Jesus said, "My thoughts are not your thoughts and my ways are not your ways' says the Lord, 'for as the heavens are higher than the earth, so are my ways higher than your ways and my thoughts than your thoughts'" (Isaiah 55:8-9). I know that's hard to comprehend. After they have offended you, Jesus tells you to go and reconcile with them. Doesn't that sound foreign? He said, "I want you to be the mature one and go to them even though they were the one who hurt you." Let's look at the other side of this scripture, "But if you do not forgive, neither will your Father which is in heaven forgive your trespasses" (Mark 11:26). "Unforgiveness is like the little foxes that spoil the vine" (Song of Solomon. 2:15). You may say, "Forgiving is hard," or "They hurt me so badly and I can't forgive." This is where God's perfect way comes into play. You forgive by faith, not by feeling. You may experience some emotional hostility towards them, but I am not talking about feelings. Feelings will come and go. All the biblical promises are activated and relative to our lives only through faith and not through feelings. It is difficult to forgive people by feelings. You want to kill them by feelings. And deal with the consequences later. You forgive by faith, by the act of your will; from your heart, not your feelings. First, you consciously, by faith, forgive and release that person of the wrong he/she committed against you.

Sometimes we are prone to think we never commit any wrongs, but we hurt others also. Sometimes we do not even know who we hurt. Many times, we do not do it intentionally but the hurt is very real to that person. Because of our inability to live without error or without inflicting hurt on others, God has provided forgiveness from sin. This was not available before Jesus, but now provision has been for you to be released from the effects of sin by faith.

Let's look at Matthew 18:21-35. Here we see Peter asking Jesus, "Lord how many times shall I forgive my brother when he sins against me up to seven times?" Jesus replied, "Forgiveness needs to be exercised largely. Not just seven times but seventy times seven," which is 490 times. Jesus meant no limits should be set. See, Jesus is not like us. After being hurt after seven times by the same person— and it's like they never seem to mature from hurting you— we are ready to kick them to the curb. Oh yes, we do! Moreover, I'm not excluded. Jesus is not saying to lie down and become a door mat for some folks. Because you know if you keep lying there they will walk all over you. No, Jesus is saying forgive, but to treat them in a different way. In addition, what I mean by that is have you ever heard the saying that you have to handle some folks with a "long-handled spoon?" Well, that's pretty much what Jesus is saying, and what He calls it is, "governmental forgiveness." For instance, after a person continues to offend you repeatedly, you go to that person telling them their fault against you. If they are still oblivious, then and only then do you handle them with a long-handle spoon. You forgive them, and you move on. However, you treat them different. Because at this point, God needs to show them a revelation of whom He is and of whom you are. Obviously, this person does not respect and treasure your relationship. Sometimes, the Holy Spirit will tell you to back up off them. Because at this point, trust has to be built back, hurts have to heal, and God and only God can take the relationship to the next level. Is anyone getting anything from this? I hope so. Only God can heal hurts and bind wounds if you so let him. God's perfect way is forgiveness. I believe the divorce rates will go down in Christians marriages if we would adhere to God's way of doing things. Relationships would mend. In addition, there could be more healing taking place in the homes, our churches would be in harmony, if we would try things God's way. However, we have so many hard hearts. Jesus spoke about God's will from the beginning, how man, because of the hardness of their hearts suffered to put away their spouses, but from the beginning it was not so. God's intent is that our relationships would endure till the end. God's intention is we would come to experience great abundance and a lasting endurance in our walk with Him and in our relationships. Moreover, this is God's perfect will.

A Spirit of Obedience

Hebrews 5:8

Talking to Pastor Walls the other day, I ask him, "Why is it that when we hear obedience we do the opposite?" He said, "Obedience has to be taught. Obedience to God's word has to be learned. You don't just automatically walk in it." The Bible said, "Jesus learn obedience by what He suffered' "Hebrews 5:8). Looking back on my own experience, that is the way I'm learning obedience by the things that I may suffer and by the voice and word of God. Our spirit is so willing to obey the voice of the Lord, but our decisions (flesh) gets in the way and detour us from doing the right thing. If Jesus had to learn obedience, then how much more shall we? We are not exempt.

Obedience is an instant response to an instruction you receive from God. You will not move pass or go forward to the next assignment until you obey the last instruction you have receive. Obedience is key to your next assignment. That's why so many Christians are frustrated or bored to tears in their walk with the Lord, they refuse to obey God. Malachi says Israel thought it was vain to serve God, that it was vain to obey His ordinances because they saw that even the wicked and the proud was set up for deliverance (Malachi 3:13-18). Whosoever shall call on the name of the Lord shall be saved. Those who obey Him shall be delivered. The Lord is no respecter of persons.

Isaiah said, "If you are willing and obedient then will you eat the good of the land. When you disobey, if you refuse and rebel you shall be devoured with the sword for the mouth of the Lord has spoken it" (Isaiah 1:19-20). Now we know that the Old Testament scripture is an example of how the Lord is true to His word. Moreover, we as New Testament saints, ought to get serious about obeying His word. The Old Testament scriptures are used as a shadow and type, an example on how the Lord dealt with those who disobeyed His word. "For those of us who willfully and continue in sin, it says, for if we sin willfully after that we have received the knowledge of the truth, there remains no more sacrifice for sin" (Hebrews 10:26). In other words, if we go on deliberately and willfully sinning (disobeying God) after once acquiring the knowledge of the truth, there is no longer any sacrifice left to atone for our sins (no further offering to which to look forward). There's nothing left for us then, but a kind of awful and fearful prospect and expectation of divine judgement and the fury of burning wrath and indignation which will consume those who put themselves in opposition to God, Hebrews 10:27). Any person who has violated and thus rejected and set at naught the law of Moses is put to death without pity or mercy on the evidence of two or three witnesses, (Hebrews 10:28). How much worst sterner and heavier punishment do you suppose he will be judged to deserve who spurned and thus trample underfoot the Son of God, and who has considered the covenant blood by which He was consecrated common and unhallowed, thus profaning it and insulting and outraging the Holy Spirit who imparts grace" (the unmerited favor and blessing of God) (Hebrews 10:26-29). For we know Him that has said, "Vengeance belongs unto me, I will recompense, says the Lord. And again, the Lord shall Judge His people, (Hebrews.10:30).

"Behold, to obey is better than sacrifice, and to hearken than the fat of rams" (1 Samuel 15:22). It is so much better to do what God says do, than trying to impress God with what we desire to do. Here, God told Samuel to tell Saul to kill all the Amalekites, utterly destroy them. But instead, Saul killed the choice animals, spared the king and kept the spoil. Was that obedience? No. When God speaks a command, even if it doesn't make since, it's not up to us to rationalize, or pick and choose what we will obey or not obey. Saul totally disobey a command from God. See, I don't think Christians take God seriously. We think by ignoring Godly instruction, that God would just forget about it. It cost Saul his kingdom, and then it cost him his life. Every time we disobey God, we allow spiritual death to creep into our members. We build strong holds (Idols)in our souls, which makes it harder each time to obey God. Nevertheless, we separate ourselves from God. When Adam and Eve disobeyed, they caused a separation from God, and they no longer could experience the Glory and fellowship with God the way they once did. That's why we are not experiencing real, true and lasting joy that passes all understanding. We have more Christians who are depressed and oppressed by the devil. That's why Jesus was manifested, to destroy the works of the devil. And we the church are supposed to imitate Jesus.

"Nevertheless, if thou shalt indeed obey His voice, and do all that I speak; then I will be an enemy unto thine enemies, and an adversary unto thine adversaries. For Mine Angel shall go before thee" (Exodus 23:22-23). See, we don't even have to fight our own battles if we would hearken to the voice of the Lord. He said, (I am paraphrasing) "I'll be a terror to your adversary."

"However, if we would not obey the voice of the Lord, but rebel against the commandment of the Lord; then shall the hand of the Lord be against you, as it was against your fathers" (1 Samuel 12:15). It's like when Pastor Moses ask the children of Israel to do something and they began to murmur and complain. They were not complaining against Moses. When they question every move Pastor Moses made, they are really questioning God. It's like when we put God on the backburner when He ask us to do something and you take your everlasting time doing it. Then we cannot expect Him to be there for you as quickly as you would like Him to be. It was not Pastor Moses that was requiring of them. It was God Himself. Moses was just a mouth piece for God (Exodus 16).

If any man will do His [Jesus'] will he shall know of the doctrine, whether it be of God, or whether I speak of myself" (John 7:17). Back in Jesus's day, He had the same problem: people accusing Him of doing His own will. Moreover, others having a problem, thinking He was preaching His own doctrine. However, if we do the will of the Father, we would know whether it was His will or the Father's. We still have folks in the church who have had problems with trusting leadership and refuse to submit to any leadership because of abuse in the past or disobedience on their part. As a result, they stay in a state of rebellion, and hurt their relationship with the Father. That's why we have restoration ministries— to restore trust, hope back into the family of God so we can trust Him. If we cannot trust the authority that we sit under, we will certainly not be able to trust God, who is our ultimate authority. "Who, being in the form of God: thought it not robbery to be equal to God but made of himself no reputation and became obedience to death even the death of the cross" (Philippians 2:6-8). He humbled himself and learned obedience by the things He suffered (Hebrews 5:8). "I, Lo, I come in the volume of the book it is written of me to do thy will, O God" (Hebrews 10:7).

Genesis. 6:22*
Genesis. 22:2*
Joshua. 11:15*
2 Kings 18:6*
Acts 26:19*
John. 14:31*
John. 15:10*
Romans. 5:19*
Matthew. 7:24*
Ephesians. 5:6*
Hebrews. 2:2-3*

Living A Life of Humility

1 Peter 5:5-6

Humility— freedom from pride, lowliness, meekness, modesty, mildness.

Peter says, "Likewise, ye younger submit yourselves unto the elder. Yea, all of you be subject to one another, and be clothed with humility; for God resist the proud and give grace to the humble." (1 Peter 5:5). "Humble yourselves therefore under the mighty hand of God, that he may exalt you in due time" (1 Peter 5:6). Church leaders were usually older members. The younger members were to place themselves willingly under the authority of those who had been given the responsibility of leadership.

Peter exhorted both young and old alike to clothe or tie oneself with humility. See we have folks in the church who do not want to sit under no body. We feel "I'm my own boss, anybody tells me what to do, you're not the boss of me. I don't feel I have to serve anyone. I have my degrees and that's beneath me." Nevertheless, the problem is there is too much of self-there. You just haven't been sanctified; you haven't been broken under the power of the Holy Ghost. Peter said be clothed with humility. See, a person that has been broken under the power of the Holy Ghost is dead. You are a dead person living the life of humility. There are some folks who think being humble, or meek is a sign of weakness and despicable, but Jesus made it the cornerstone of character. However, God says if you humble yourself, I'll give you anything You ask of me. The scripture did say the meek shall inherit the earth. A meek person is not weak, meekness is not weakness, it is "strength under control." For God says in that same verse that He resist the proud, He opposes the proud, the arrogant, but grants favor and acceptance to the humble. To humble ourselves is a condition of God's favor. How many wants the favor of God on his/her life? Then live a life of humility. You can't live this life apart from the Holy Spirit. God humbles men to bring them to obedience (Deuteronomy.8:2). You do not ever want to experience the Lord having to humble you. Peter says, "Humble yourselves under the mighty hand of God, that he may exalt you in due time." That can mean to allow yourself to be humbled. Those who were suffering persecution for Christ sake could be encouraged by the fact that the same mighty hand that allow them to suffer would one day lift (exalt) them up. "Humble yourselves in the sight of the Lord, and He shall lift you up" (James 4:10).

Moreover, to the spirit filled women, there are those who are going into marriage and ministry, so you have to be clothed with humility. You are entering into a completely new realm of humility. Ephesians 5:21-24 says, "Submitting yourselves one to another in the fear of God. Wives, submit yourselves unto your own husbands. As unto the Lord." So, wives, you are actually rendering services unto the Lord and obeying what He has set up and ordained. Submission does not mean that she is owned and operated by her husband but that he is "head or manager." This is a truly liberated women. Submission is God's design for women. Christ's example teaches that true submission is neither reluctant nor grudging, nor is it a result of imposed authority; it is rather an act of worship to God when it is chosen, deliberate, voluntary response to a husband.

In Philippians, the second chapter, Jesus was in total submission to the Father and gave up every right He had. He did not lose His identity.

On the contrary, He knew exactly who He was and for what purpose He was on earth. Even though He became a servant in human form, He knew that He was the son of God equal with God the Father. You know in the God head there exist perfect unity, equality, and harmony. Submission is not a status of inferiority. No way can you live this life aside from God. You have to be filled with the Holy Spirit. The scripture says, not to be drunk with wine but be filled with His precious Holy Ghost. Moreover, even if you are, you have to yield yourself to the Lord on a daily basis so that Christ can live through you. Paul says, "I am crucified with Christ; nevertheless, I live; yet not I, but Christ lives in me; and the life which I now live in the flesh I live by the faith of the Son of God, who loved me and gave himself for me" (Galatians 2:20)

Saying all of that let's take a look at false humility. Colossians 2:18 says, "Let no man beguile or mislead you of your reward in a voluntary humility, for instance, submitting to someone who claims to be superior because of special visions who insist on false humility, worshiping of angels, intruding into those things which he hath not seen, vainly puffed up by his fleshly mind. Such a person is puffed up by his human way of thinking (pride). For instance, a heretic is one who turns believers away from faithful service and has false humility, which is only a "form of godliness but denying it's power" (2 Timothy 3:5). Such a person is puffed up by his human way of thinking (pride). I believe in the gifts of God more than the next person does. Moreover, I love to see the nine gifts of the Spirit move and Flow in the body of Christ when it's done in order by the biding of the Holy Spirit. Nevertheless, there are those who are going around with "parking lot prophecies," (false prophecy) thinking they have special visions from the Lord, making others in the body think that they have special gift from the Lord. But the scripture said, "If you continue in my word then are you my disciples indeed and you shall know the truth, and the truth shall make you free" (John 8:31-32). Did you catch that? If you continue in the word, you would be disciplined enough to know it. He did not say, if you get a dose of the word. He said, if you "continue." That means to constantly go after more of God. Sunday morning Christians get only a dose, and that's why so many of them are in bondage. You are in bondage to flesh. You are in bondage to tradition and self-righteousness. If you are consistently in the word of God, you'll recognize it when you hear it. You won't be tossed about by every wind of doctrine. You won't be easily influenced by the wrong thing. When someone tells you something that doesn't line up with the word of God, you dismiss it instead of falling prey to it. So many people are misled by unfounded prophecies and visions. When you meet people, who claim to speak for God, find out if they've been tested and proven. Seasoned saints have something to impart to your life. A true prophet brings a life-changing experience with them. Proven prophecies should bring about real change.

The Love of God

John 3:16

When we think of the "love of God" we somehow think of it from our advantage or point of view. We always see ourselves on the receiving end. Love is not love until we decided to give it away. Sure, we have to learn to love ourselves before we can love another. The Bible says to love your neighbor as you love yourself.

Love is not a feeling, but it is something that we decide to do. Paul said that while we were yet sinners Christ (demonstrated) His love; He died for the ungodly. It was a decision that He made. No, He didn't feel like dying. It was love in action personified. In other words, Christ represented God while He died on the cross to demonstrate how much He loved us saying, "I love you enough to die, I love you enough to suffer, I love you enough to despise the shame and to endure the cross." No, He didn't feel like it. He went to God in the Garden of Gethsemane three times asking, "Is there another way?" saying, "Let this cup of suffering pass from me, but never the less not mine will, but let thine will be done." Therefore, love is an action that we decide to do because in life we will encounter all kinds of people and personalities. And if our love is not rooted and grounded in God so that we can comprehend what is the length, depth and height of love, then we will get discouraged from loving again. When you come into the revelation of God's love and began to experience the mysteries of God's love, then you will know how to walk in it, as well as know how to demonstrate it. For instance, "God so loved the world that He gave His only begotten son, that whosoever believes in Him shall not perish but have everlasting life" (John 3:16). Here, God extends His love to the entire world. Now He says "whosoever believes." Now there's a condition placed on receiving His love; it's that you have to believe. Moreover, there's a promise that is given after you meet the condition. The promise is that you will have eternal life, not just in the here and after, but in the here and now. Moreover, once we received the promise of His love, then we have ever lasting life, and the power and ability to give that same love that was demonstrated to us, we have the power to give it to somebody else. We can't give love away if we never experienced the God kind of love for ourselves. In addition, that's why it's so hard for people to love. That's why folks have conditional love instead of unconditional love, with strings attached, looking for something in return. They can't give something away that they never had. Try loving someone who never experienced the God kind of love. They are incapable of loving you back. They don't know how. Let's look at scriptures on the "God kind of love".

No matter how many gifts and talents we have, if we are not operating in love, then our gifts are good for nothing. If we are puffed up in pride and arrogance, then we can speak in tongues, we can prophecy, we can give our bodies to be burned, it's all in vain if we don't exercise love, it's as good for nothing.

Love endures long; love is patient and kind; love is not envious nor boils over in jealousy; is not boastful or vainglorious, does not display itself haughtily. It's not conceited (arrogant and inflated with pride); it is not rude (unmannerly) and does not act unbecomingly. God's love in us does not insist on its own rights or its own way, for it is not self-seeking; it is not touchy or fretful or resentful; it takes no account of the evil done to it; it pays no attention to a suffered wrong). It does not rejoice at injustice and unrighteousness but rejoices when right and truth prevail. Love bears up under anything and everything that comes, is ever ready to believe the best of every person, its hopes are fadeless under all circumstances, and it endures everything (without weakening).

Love never fails: But whether there be prophecies, they shall fail; whether there be tongues, they shall cease; whether there be knowledge, it shall vanish away. Love never fails (never out or becomes obsolete or comes to and end) 1Corinthians 13:1-8.

Let love be without dissimulation, I abhor that which is evil; and cleave to that which is good. Let your love be sincere [a real love] hate what is evil [loath all ungodliness, turn in horror from wickedness], but hold fast to that which is good. Be kindly affectioned one to another with brotherly love; in honor preferring one another. Love one another with brotherly love and affection as members of one family giving precedence. Romans 12:9-10

Love works no ill to his neighbor; therefore, love is the fulfilling of the law. Love does no wrong to one's neighbor [it never hurts anybody]. Romans 13:10 AMP

"For the love of Christ constrains me; because I thus judge, that if one died for all, then were all dead." (2 Corinthians. 5:14). For the love of God controls and urges and impels us, because we are of the opinions and conviction that if one died for all, then all died. The more you love the Lord the more you don't do the things that will offend or grieve Him. The more we love Jesus, the more we operate in self-control.

"Beloved, let us love one another: for love is of God; and every one that loves is born of God, and knows God" (1 John 4:7).

Beloved, let us love one another, for love is [springs] from God; and he who loves [his fellowman] is begotten [born] of God and is coming [progressively] to know and understand God to [perceive and recognize and get a better and clearer knowledge of Him] 1 John 4:7.

"For in Jesus Christ neither circumcision avails anything nor uncircumcision; but faith, which works by love" (Galatians 5:6).

"For (if we are) in Christ Jesus, neither circumcision nor uncircumcision count for anything but only faith activated and energized and expressed and working through love" (Galatians 5:6).

The Fruit of The Spirit

Galatians 5:19-26

Now the works of the flesh are manifest, which are these, adultery, fornication, uncleanness, lasciviousness, Idolatry, witchcraft, hatred, variance, emulations, wrath strife seditions, heresies, envying, murder, drunkenness, reveling, and such like: of the which I tell you before, as I have also told you in times past, that they which do such things shall not inherit the kingdom of God," (Galatians 5:19).

However, the fruit of the Spirit is love, joy, peace, longsuffering, gentleness, goodness, faith, meekness temperate: against such there is no law. And they that are Christ's have crucified the flesh with the affections and lust. If we live in the Spirit, let us also walk in the Spirit. Let us not be desirous of vain glory, provoking one another, envying one another" (Galatians 5:22-26).

In verse 19, starting with the works of the flesh, these are what we call sins that originate from the sinful nature, the "Adamic nature" and not with the new nature indwell by the Holy Spirit. These are obvious sins, meaning public and cannot be hidden. The first three sexual sins are mention. Sexual immorality is often translated fornication. From this word comes "pornography". Porneia refers to any and all forms of illicit sexual relationships. Impurity is a broad term referring to moral uncleanness in thought, word, and deed. Debauchery imply an open, shameless, brazen display of these evils, meaning anything goes. In addition, some of us are comfortable operating in these things. See, if I don't expose these sins, some of you will continue in them like it's nothing. The very fact that we feel comfortable watching soft porn on cable is a indication that we are comfortable in these things. Oh, you may say, "Well, I didn't commit any act; I was just watching it." See, that's how sin starts off, with a seed planted in your heart, and then before you know you're thinking about it all the time. Our teens are engaging in immorality, sins unto death. Our kids are dying of AIDS, and we, as parents, are standing by watching it happen. "Well, I'm just supporting my son because I love him." You can love your son, but not the sin they are doing. Don't support sin. Following the sexual sins Paul tells us about the two religious sins, Idolatry, involving worshiping of pagan gods by bowing to them. In today's society we may not have little wooden gods to bow to, but we bow to humanism, in the church, putting our agenda before God, not seeking the Lord before we proceed with our plans and programs. Moreover, we did that last year, and the Lord really blessed us, so we try to do the same thing again without consulting God. Witchcraft, the word witchcraft is derived from the Greek word, pharmakeia, which means drugs. In ancient times practitioners of witchcraft used drugs to induce people to worship idols. In today's society, we operate in these things to seduce others with manipulation, deception, and control, Why? Because we want our own way, we want to control others. It's a form of witchcraft, rebellion. Hatred, discord, jealousy, envy, drunkenness, orgies and the like— Paul says those who continue in these things will not inherit the future kingdom of God.

Let's look at the nine fruits of the Spirit. There is something beautiful about love, is that all nine fruit stems from love. The reason love is the first fruit mentioned is because all the other fruit flow through love. 1 Corinthians 13:4 says: Love is kind, it does not envy, it does not boast, it is not proud, it's not rude, it's not self-seeking, it is not easily angered, it keeps no records of wrongs. Love does not delight in evil but rejoices with the truth. It always protects, always trust, always hopes, always perseveres.

Joy; you know you can't have joy without first displaying the fruit of love. Remember, joy stems from love. Joy is an inward stability, it's not based on the circumstances around you. It can hold its own. I can have joy whether you like me or not, it doesn't matter, I still have the joy of the Lord. Peace is the umpire of the soul. You can display peace when all hell is breaking loose, you can still have peace, that passes all understanding whose minds are stayed on thee. Longsuffering; this the fruit of perseverance, standing until you see the fulfilment of your prayers coming through. Gentleness; the Greek word for gentleness is chrestotes, and it means kindness. The scripture shares that God is kind, nature is kind, God's judgements are kind, and His instructions are kind, therefore we can be kind. Goodness derived from the Greek word kalos and agathos. Kalos means appealing to the eyes; agathos means holy and moral. We all know that we serve a good God, God is good all the time. "It's the goodness of the Lord that leads us to repentance" (Romans 2:4). Faith; in previous chapters we learned there are three kinds of faith: 1.) faith to become a born-again child of God, 2.) a supernatural kind of faith given to help you during difficult circumstances, 3.) the fruit of faithfulness which comes from your reborn human spirit. Faithfulness is a characteristic of our Heavenly Father. It is so important to remain faithful. Faithful in our walk; in our lifestyle, marriages, church, and friends. Meekness does not mean you're spineless, that everybody walks on, it means you are self-controlled. Numbers 12:3 states, "Moses was very meek, above all the men, which were upon the face of the earth." Moses was not weak, he was self- controlled. Temperance after you have learned self-control, God wants us to be temperate. 1 Corinthians 9:25 describes this last fruit: "And every man that strives for mastery is temperate in all things. Now they do it to obtain a corruptible crown; but we an incorruptible." This scripture is saying, to be a winner we should be temperate in all things. People who are well-disciplined in their spiritual walk are successful Christians and that pleases God.

Walking in the Character of the Holy Spirit

Galatians 3:2-3

Let me ask you this one question. Did you receive the Holy Spirit as a result of "obeying the law and doing its work, or was it by hearing the message of the gospel and believing it?" (Galatians 3:2). "Are you so foolish?" (Galatians 3:3). Having begun in the Spirit, are ye now made perfect by the flesh? In other words, Paul is asking a rhetorical question: How did you receive the Holy Spirit? Paul is saying if you receive the Lord by faith, then why you are trying to become mature by your works? The same way you were saved and walk in the spirit, you did it by faith; then that's what it will take to get mature in your faith. It points toward their conversions of the Galatians when they received the Holy Spirit. Thus, Paul did not question their salvation but challenged them to consider whether they were saved and received the Spirit by faith or because of works. It was, of course, by faith when they heard Paul preach the Gospel. So, you may ask, "Well, Minister Walls, it sounds like to me that Paul is contradicting the book of James where it says that, 'What doth it profit, my brethren, though a man say he hath faith, and have not works, can faith save him?'"

If a brother or sister be naked, and destitute of daily food, and one of you say unto them, depart in peace, be ye warmed filled; notwithstanding ye give them not those things which are needful to the body what doth it profit? Even so faith, if it hath not works, is dead being alone. James 2:14-17.

On the other hand, Paul says that "if you receive the Lord by faith then why you are trying to become mature by your works?" (Galatians 3:2).

Here, Paul is not saying that we can't operate by works, but it has to be through faith. For instance, it has to be at the bidding or request of the Lord. We have to obey the voice of the Lord (prompting of the Holy Spirit), not do things the way we think that it should be and then ask the Lord to bless it. When we trust the Lord, we consult him, we put him first, and we make him first priority in everything, not trusting in ourselves the way we are so accustomed. What God want us to do is to start living from our spirit and not from our heads. To obey the promptings of the Holy Spirit is to obey God. That comes with constant fellowship with God. When you consistently fellowship with God, you become acquainted with him. You begin to know of his ways, and you find out that they are so different from our ways (Isaiah 55: 8-9). The Bible teaches us that Jesus's prayer life was amazing. He prayed and ministered to people all day. Then he prayed all night, fellowshipping with the Father. The Scriptures say that he got up a great while before dawn to pray. Jesus kept his flesh under submission by praying, spending time with the Father. That is exactly what he told his disciples to do. "Pray lest you enter into temptation."

To know the character of the Holy Spirit, it begins by walking in the Spirit. Another way of walking in the Spirit is that we have to learn of God's ways and begin to do things his way and not our own way. Romans 6:11-14 says:

> Likewise reckon [settling of accounts; take into consideration] ye yourselves to be dead in deed unto sin, but alive unto God

through Jesus Christ our Lord. Let not sin therefore reign in your mortal body, that ye should obey it in the lust thereof. Neither yield your members as instruments of unrighteousness unto sin: but yield yourselves unto God, as those that are alive from the dead, and your members as instrument to righteousness unto God. For sin shall not have dominion over you: for ye are not under the law, but under grace.

When you are born again, you no longer have to be dominated by sin. You are recreated to live in the spiritual realm of God. You can walk in the spirit while you are here on the earth. "Know you not, that to whom ye yield yourselves servants to obey, his servants ye are to whom ye obey?" (Romans 6:16). You walk in the spirit by yielding to and obeying the promptings of your spirit instructed by the Holy Spirit. That's why I love baby Christians; they hear these promptings by the Holy Spirit and just do it because God loves spontaneity. They don't wait until they can analyze, reason, have logic, and understand the Word; they believe by faith and act on it, unlike others whom you have to convince and persuade (beg and plead with them) before they would even begin to do what the Lord is requiring of them.

THE GIFTS OF THE SPIRIT

I Corinthians 12:1-11

I. The Gift of the Word of Wisdom

Definition:

> The Gift of the Word of Wisdom is the revealing of God's wisdom (fragment, portion) regarding the future under the anointing of God.

Scripture Example:

> God revealed in three of David's psalms how the Messiah would come and how He (the Messiah) would die. This was a revelation of the future (Psalms 2 and 22).

Explanation:

> David had spoken this word of wisdom even before it had ever taken place, of Jesus and his coming and dying on the cross.

II. The Gift of the Word of Knowledge

Definition:

> The Gift of the Word of Knowledge is the revealing of a fact in existence which cannot be seen, heard or revealed naturally. It is in existence, it is a fact (past of present), it is knowledge and it is supernaturally revealed by God.

Scripture Example:

> "When he (Jesus) saw Nathaniel, he said "...Behold an Israelite indeed, in whom is no guile! Whence knowest thou me? Jesus answered and said unto him (Nathaniel), Before that Philip called thee, when thou wast under the fig tree, I saw thee," (John 1:47-50).

Explanation:

> Here, supernaturally, the Lord Jesus Christ saw this man the day before sitting under a fig tree. This was the word of God's knowledge.

III. The Gift of Special Faith

Definition:

> The Gift of Special Faith is when God imparts (special) faith to a person to enable that person to stand amidst devastating circumstances. That person would not be able to stand without this spontaneous burst of special faith. It is over and above salvation faith and ordinary faith. Even though all things of

God are received by faith, this Gift of Special Faith is a special supernatural faith imparted for that specific stance.

Scripture Example:

> Daniel 3:20-21 says, "Then these men were bound in their coats, their hosen, and their hats and their other garments, and were cast into the midst of the burning fiery furnace."

Explanation:

> When the three Hebrew boys were placed in the fiery furnace, they did not fight the flames. They did not resist the flames. They did not put out the fire. God supernaturally preserved them.

IV. The Gifts of Healing

Definition:

> The Gifts of Healing is when God works through one of His spirit-filled vessels imparting a supernatural healing to another or others. There is no outside aid whatsoever. No pills, no radiation, no operation, etc. This healing is usually spontaneous. A person is sick one minute and instantly healed the next. No healing process. Because it serves as an advertisement for God, it is not always the saved who get healed, but many times the unsaved. As a result, they are drawn to God. God has a way!

Scripture Example:

> Luke 8:43 says, "and a woman having an issue of blood twelve years, which had spent all her living upon physicians, neither could be healed of any."

Explanation:

> The woman with an issue of blood who had suffered for twelve years, even though she had been treated by many doctors. She had spent all her money, but instead of getting better she got worse all the time. She had heard about Jesus, so she came in the crowd behind him saying within herself, "If I just touch his clothes, I will get well." And when she touched Jesus' garment Jesus had perceived that virtue (or power) had gone from him. This was the Gift of Healing in operation. The woman's bleeding had immediately stopped.

V. The Gift of the Working of Miracles

Definition:

> The Gift of the Working of Miracles is the supernatural intervention by God in the ordinary course of nature. In this Gift, God performs through a person or through some instrument a miracle or a happening here on earth beyond any human capability or strength.

Scripture Example:

> God performs through David in 1 Samuel 17:34-37; and 37 reads, "David said, "Moreover, the Lord that delivered me out of the paw of the lion and out of the paw of the bear, he will deliver me out of the hand of this Philistine. And Saul said unto David, Go, and the Lord be with thee."

Explanation:

> When David slew a lion and a bear with his naked hands, it was "the working of miracles." As we all know, you cannot destroy a lion or a bear with your bare hands!

VI. The Gift of Prophecy

Definition:

> The Gift of Prophecy is the anointed speaking forth in the God-given natural tongue words of edification, exhortation, or comfort to the church, supernaturally given from God without human thinking.

Scripture Example:

> "If any man speak in an unknown tongue, let it be by two, or at the most by three, and that by course; and let one interpret" (1 Corinthians 14:27).

Explanations:

> This Gift of Prophecy is to be regulated. Only three prophecies are allowed in any one meeting.

VII. The Gift of Discerning of Spirits

Definition:

> The Gift of Discerning of Spirits is when the Holy Spirit enables one to see into the spirit world. That person can comprehend

supernaturally the spirit at work in another person. But remember, only as he, the Holy Spirit, wills.

Scripture Example:

In Acts 8:20-23, Peter looked at Simon and said "Thy money perish with thee, because thou has thought that the gift of God may be purchased with money. Thou has neither part nor lot in this matter. For thy heart is not right in the sight of God. Repent therefore of this thy wickedness, and pray God, if perhaps the thought of thine heart may be forgiven thee. For I perceive that thou art in the gall of bitterness and in the bond of iniquity.

Explanation:

An example of the use of this gift is found in Acts 8:28. Simon (the sorcerer) looked on with wonder as Peter and John laid hands on people and they would receive the Holy Ghost. Simon thought in his heart, "If only I had such power it would make me a big man among people. Every man had his price. I will persuade these men to sell this power to me." So he offered the apostles money. Peter had to discern this thing in Simon's heart.

VIII. The Gift of Divers Kinds of Tongues

Definition:

The Gift of Tongues is when God uses one of His Spirit filled vessels in that new language he has imparted unto him/her in the speaking forth to a congregation. As the congregation listens, the gift of tongues will be followed by interpretation which will edify, comfort and exhort that congregation. For you see, the Gift of Tongues plus interpretation equals the Gift of Prophecy.

Scripture Example:

> Acts 2:4 says, "and they were all filled with the Holy Ghost, and began to speak with other tongues, as the Spirit gave them utterance."

Explanation:

> Only Spirit-filled baptized Christians are candidates for this gift. One has to first experience Acts 2:4.

IX. The Gift of Interpretation of Tongues

Definition:

> The Gift of the Interpretation of Tongues is the supernatural showing forth by the Spirit the meaning of an utterance spoken by a person in a language given by the Spirit of God, which is completely incomprehensible to the spokesman (which he does not and cannot understand with his finite mind).

Scripture Example:

> 1 Corinthians 14:4, "He that speaketh in an unknown tongue edified himself; but he that prophesieth edifieth the church."

Explanation:

> The main ministry of the Gift of Interpretation of Tongues is to edify the church. We see this because this gift must function with its sister gift, the Gift of Tongues.

X. The Ministry of the Prophet

Definition:

> The ministry of the prophet foretells the mind of God unto a specific congregation or people regarding the future. One of the confirming factors is that a person has been called by God as a prophet and that the Gift of the Word of Wisdom (which is future) will frequent his/her ministry.

Scripture Example:

> 1 Kings 18:41 - "and Elijah said unto Ahab, get thee up, eat and drink; for there is a sound of abundance of rain."

Explanation:

> This was fulfilled in 1 Kings 18:45, "and it came to pass in the meanwhile, that the heaven was black with clouds and wind, and there was a great rain. And Ahab rode, and went to Jezreel."

God's Divine Unity

Psalms 133, John 15:1-11, Acts 2:41-47, Acts 4:31, John 17:21-23

I remember a quote Rodney King said while being brutally arrested by the California Police saying, "Can't we just all get alone?" It may have seemed funny at the time to those in the media because they use it as a joke, and the world deems it as impossible to happen. Nevertheless, the Lord expects unity from the Church. David wrote, "How good and how pleasant it is for brethren to dwell together in unity" (Psalms 133:1).

Living in "divine unity" does not mean that we cannot have our own opinions about anything, but it does mean that there is "harmony mutual respect, and honor in our relationships. It means there is an absence of things that causes division and strife- like selfishness, resentment, anger, jealously, bitterness, independence or comparison.

A.) Selfishness— excessively or exclusively concerned with one's own well-being. Notice the prefix is self. Every step towards self- sufficiency is a step away from God.

B.) Resentment— feel or show annoyance at; disturb or irritated by. Which is a form of judging others.

C.) Anger— feelings of showing rage or resentment: an angry look.

D.) Jealously— suspicious of rival (competitor) of one believed to enjoy an advantage.
E.) Bitterness— extremely harsh or resentful.
F.) Independence— will not allow one-self to be governed by another. Every step towards self- sufficiency is a step away from God.
G.) Comparison— act of comparing; an adjective or adverb to show difference in levels of quality, quantity or relation. We analyze others by comparing one with another.

The devil does not have a chance if we will just be obedient to God. When we walk in the spirit, we agree with God. If I am in agreement with God. If I am in agreement with God and you are in agreement with God, we will automatically be in agreement with each other. If we will walk after the Spirit, we are going to agree with each other, because we are agreeing with the Holy Spirit. By the Spirit of God, the unity of our faith becomes a reality. We are learning to agree with God in the Spirit!

Agreement in prayer is the sum total of unity in the faith, when we are standing on the same foundations of faith, when our hearts and minds are in harmony with a purpose and a vision that we are following for the greater good. It is not to get what "we want." That is why many times, we could be in agreement with someone who really does not agree with us and our prayers are non and invalid. There is no unity and no agreement.

"While I was with them in the world, I kept them in thy name: those that thou gave me I have kept, and none of them is lost, but the son of perdition; that the scripture might be fulfilled (John17:12). Neither pray I for these alone, but for them also which shall believe on me through their word; that they all may be one; as thou, Father, art in me, and in thee, that they also may be one in us: that the world may believe that thou hast sent me. And the glory which thou gave me I have given them; that they may be one, even as we are one" (John 17:20-22). Why did Jesus pray for their preservation? (rescuing or keeping safe from death, injury, or decay). "It was to promote the unity of the believers, patterned after the unity of the Father and the Son: so that they may be one as we are one." See, what the Lord is during with us is patterning our lives after the Father and the Son. Moreover, it's for His will and His purpose not for our own. By being protected from the world, they would be unified in their desires to serve and glorify the Son. Now if you are in it for self, then you'll not glorifying the Son; you are glorifying yourself and what you can get out of it. What's in this thing for me? The disciples ask the same thing. "We have left all to follow you." And Jesus answered and said: "Verily I say unto you, there is no man that hath left houses, or brethren, or sister, or father, or mother, or wife, or children, or lands, for my sake, and the gospel's, but he/she shall receive and hundredfold now in this time, houses, and brethren, and sisters, and mothers, and children, and lands, with persecutions; and in the world to come eternal life" (Mark 10: 28-30). Therefore, there are benefits in serving God, in being unified with His Spirit. As the Good Shepherd, Jesus took care of the Flock entrusted to Him by the Father.

The final portion of Jesus' prayer was for future believers who would come to Him through the message of the Apostles. In the church age all Christians have come to Christ directly or indirectly through the Apostles' witness. Jesus knew His mission would succeed. He would send forth the Spirit, the Apostles would preach, people would be converted, and the church would be formed.

We see in verse 21 Jesus is requested unity for future believers. And you ask, "Well, how do we get unified when everyone is doing their own thing, when you have some who haven't made up their minds to whether or not they even want the demands in which the Holy Spirit requires to live in conformity to holiness, and in sync with the Lord's will and purpose?" Moreover, in order to get unified in the Church it has to take place individually. In order to follow in line with the Holy Spirit, you have to obey His instruction. "All believers belong to the one Body of Christ" (1 Corinthians 12:13), and their spiritual unity is to be manifest in the way they live. In addition, you have to come to a place where you want to get serious about Christ the Anointed One. The unity Christ desires for His Church is the same kind of unity the Son has with the Father: just as "you are in me and I am in you." The Father did His works through the Son and the Son always did what pleased the Father. This spiritual unity is to be patterned in the Church. Without union with Jesus and the Father (they... in us), Christians can do nothing: (John 15:5). The goal of their lives is to do the Father's will. Jesus was not praying here that we would unify ourselves to an institution or some building, but He was praying that we would become intimate with Him and with the Father and with the Holy Spirit and that we would have unity in love, a unity of obedience to God and His word, and a united commitment to His will.

To sum it all up is that we would fall in love with the Lord all over again. When you began to meditate on the goodness of Jesus and all He has done in your life, how He raised you, and kept you, and never left you; how He has been there for you when you couldn't find no one to be by your side; that's when my soul cries, "Hallelujah! Praise God for saving me!" When we were without hope in the world God sent a savior who would die in my stead. Jesus came through forty- two generations, was willing to die on Calvary, and go down to set the captives free. He took the keys, unlocked the grave, took the sting out of death, and gave us victory. He rose with all power in His hands and now Jesus is seated at the right hand of the Father making intercession, for you and for me, and He bought forth unity! Thanks be unto God, which gives us the victory through our Lord Jesus Christ" (1Corinthians 15:57)!

Afterword

In this part of the Western hemisphere, we, the Christian society, are searching to find out who we are. "We have these treasures in earthen vessels that the excellency of the power may be of God and not of ourselves," (2 Corinthians 4:7). In other words, we have the answer locked up inside of us. We keep looking out externally for whom we are and comparing ourselves among ourselves and keep coming up empty when God has given us everything that pertains to life and godliness. He has blessed us with every spiritual blessing in heavenly places (Ephesians 1:3). Nevertheless, the only way to know who we are is to look from within to discover ourselves and destiny through our Lord and Savior, Jesus Christ.

God has a unique purpose for you to do, one that no one here on earth can bring to pass and fulfill but you. Isn't that exciting? The problem is how are you going to fulfill it? Well, God created you; He is your source. When you go to the car dealer and purchase an automobile and you begin to have problems with it, where do you go? Back to the dealer or the source. Well, it is the same in the spiritual world; you go back to your source, and He will begin to give instructions on how to fulfill your destiny. You would have to seek him daily and begin to "wait on God," for everything so that He can begin to direct you in life for the plans that he has already designed for you. Know that there is no failure in God; He has the perfect plan for you, one that you can depend on for the rest of your life. It's an eternal plan. You are just getting ready for what you will be doing throughout eternity.

You may ask, "Well, how will He give me a new plan for my life? I have already failed and done everything. This sounds too good to be true." Well, if you have tried everything, now begin to try God and His plans that He has for you. You have nothing to lose and everything to gain. Try things His way and begin to persevere until you begin to see things happen in your life. Don't give up at the first sign of trouble. For those who put their hands to the plow and look back are not fit for the kingdom of God. The Scripture said, "Wait on the Lord: be of good courage, and He shall strengthen thy heart: wait, I say, on the Lord" (Psalms 27:14).

When I came into the knowledge of Jesus Christ, I had no idea that I would be doing any of what I'm doing now. Nevertheless, when I said yes to Jesus, He began to take me onto another road that I had never traveled before. It's called the "the way of holiness." "For the unclean shall not pass over it; but it shall be for those [the redeemed] wayfaring men, though fools, shall not err therein" (Isaiah 35:8). See, the Scripture said that there would be a way already made for you. For the redeemed, "Every valley shall be exalted, and every mountain and hill shall be made low: and the crooked shall be made straight, and the rough places plain" (Isaiah 40:4). The only thing we have to do is just choose his way of doing things. It may seem unfamiliar to those who haven't been this way, but the Holy Spirit will minister to you all the way. He will never leave you comfortless.

The only thing that the Lord requires is that you would put your total trust and faith in him. If you have not received Jesus as your Lord and Savior, begin to pray this simple prayer with me. "Dear Jesus, thank you for showing me your plans for salvation and that you are mindful of me and my whole life and welfare. Please forgive me for doing things my way, for your Word says 'There is none that seek you, all have gone out of the way' (Romans 3:11-12). Lord, I desire to make you my Lord and Savior and that you would be my guide in this life. Please put me on this road called holiness so that I can spend eternity with you. In Jesus' name, Amen!

Praise God! If you have prayed that prayer with me, then are you on your way to receiving your destiny in life. Begin to read the Word of God for further instructions from the living God, and always assemble yourself with the believers in a local, Word-based church. God bless you!

Family Photos

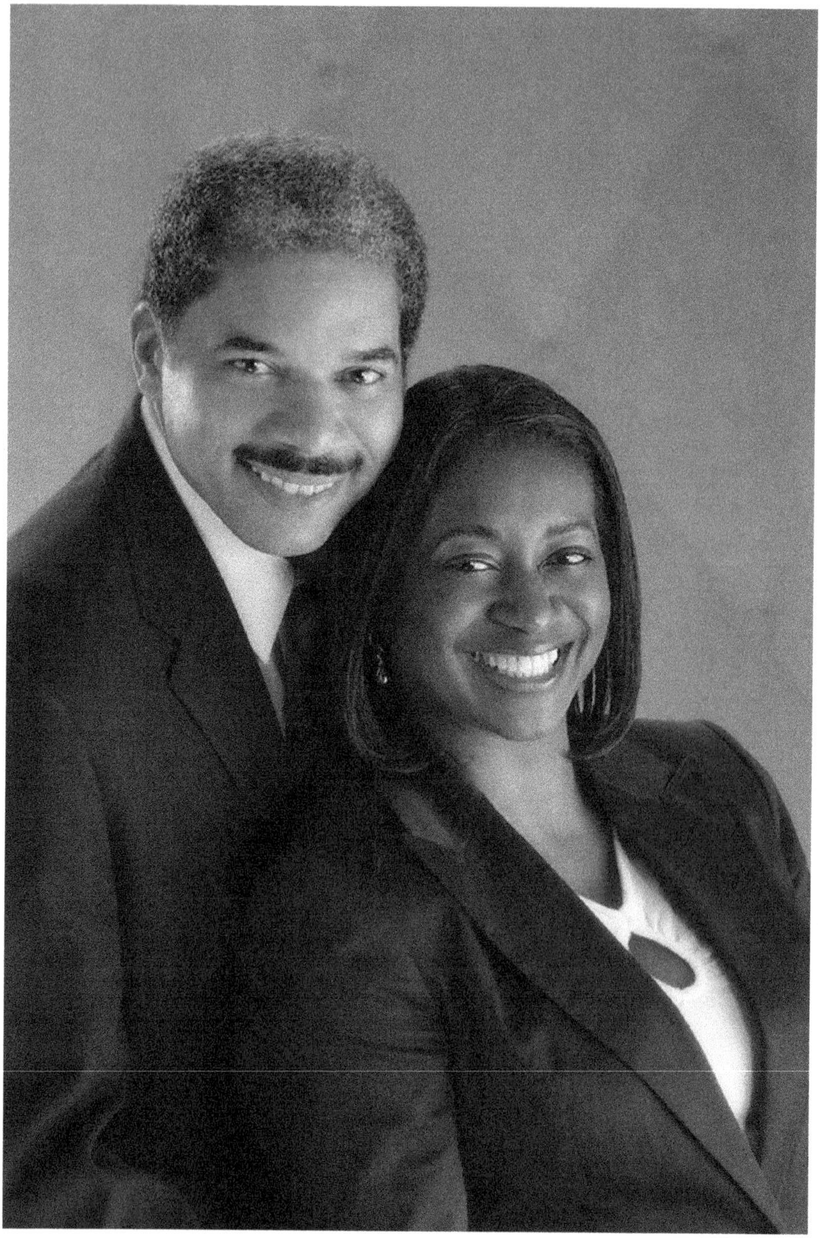

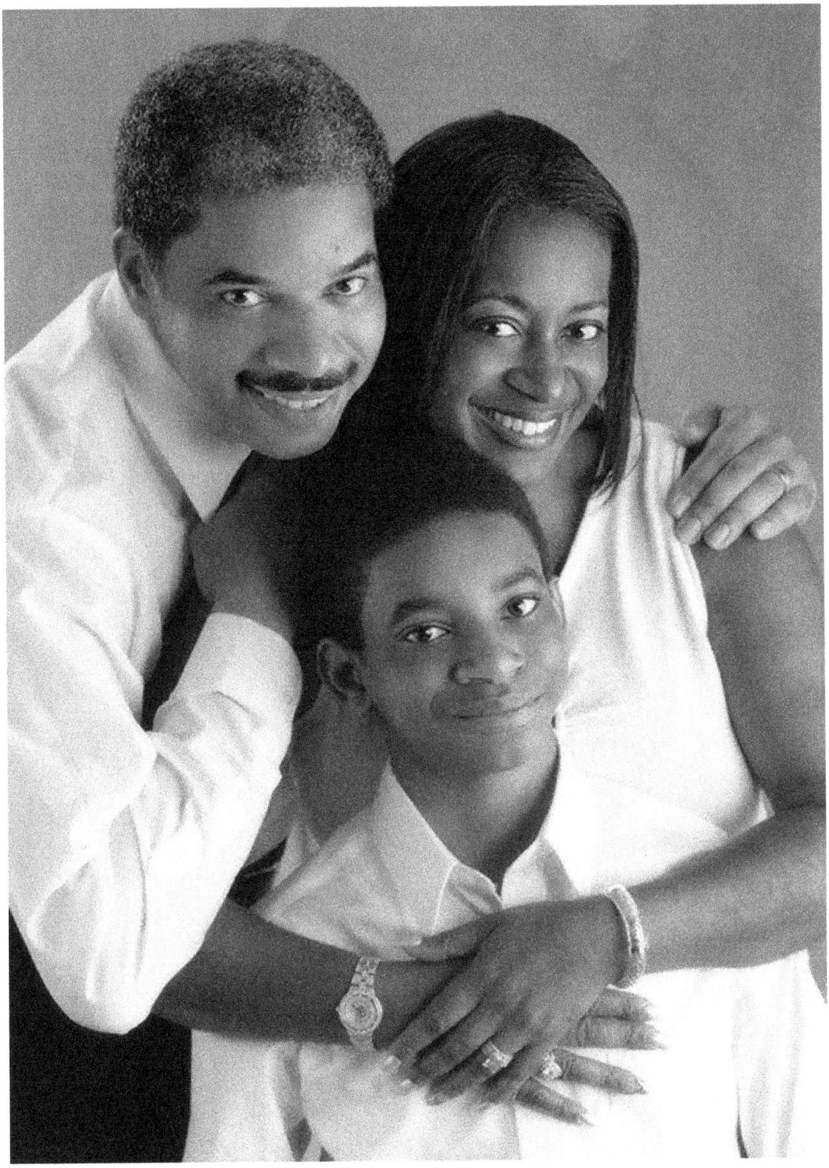

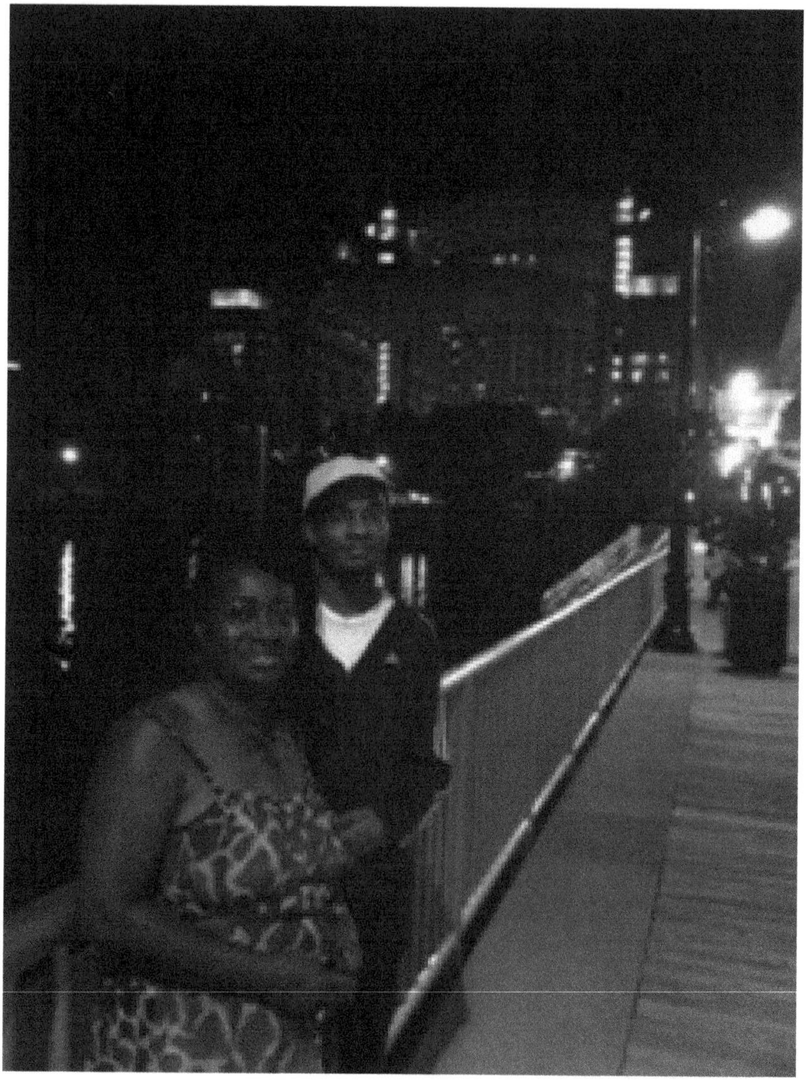

Lord Show Me Your Purpose | 125

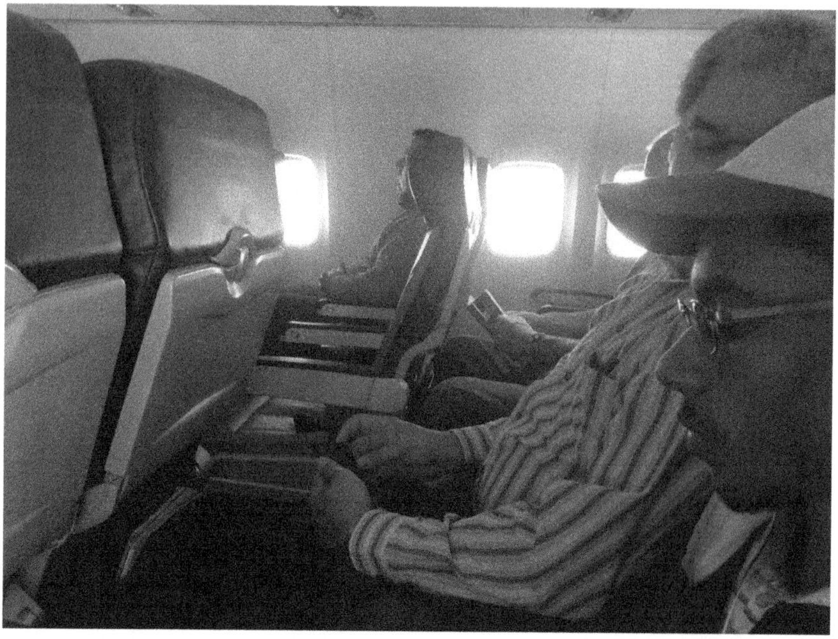

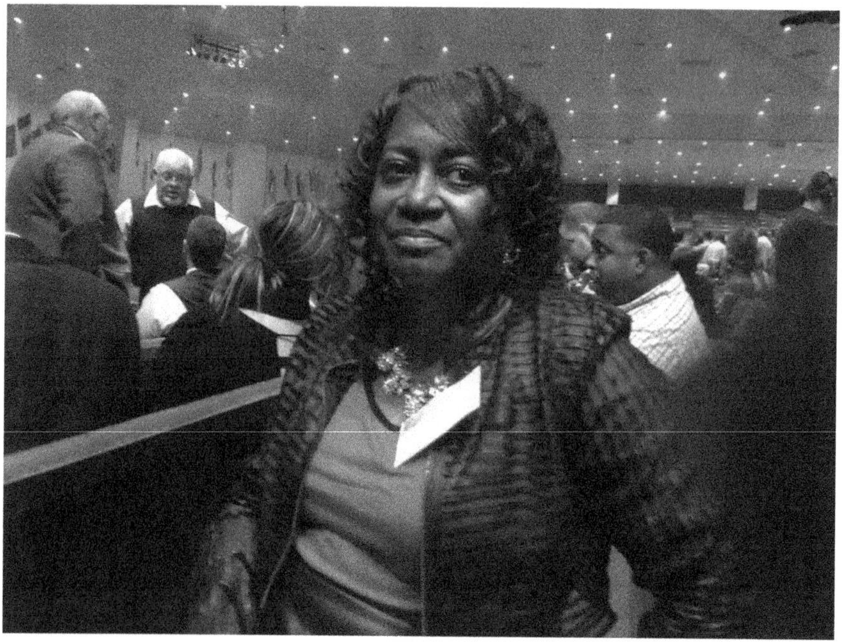

Lord Show Me Your Purpose | **127**

128 | Teresa Walls

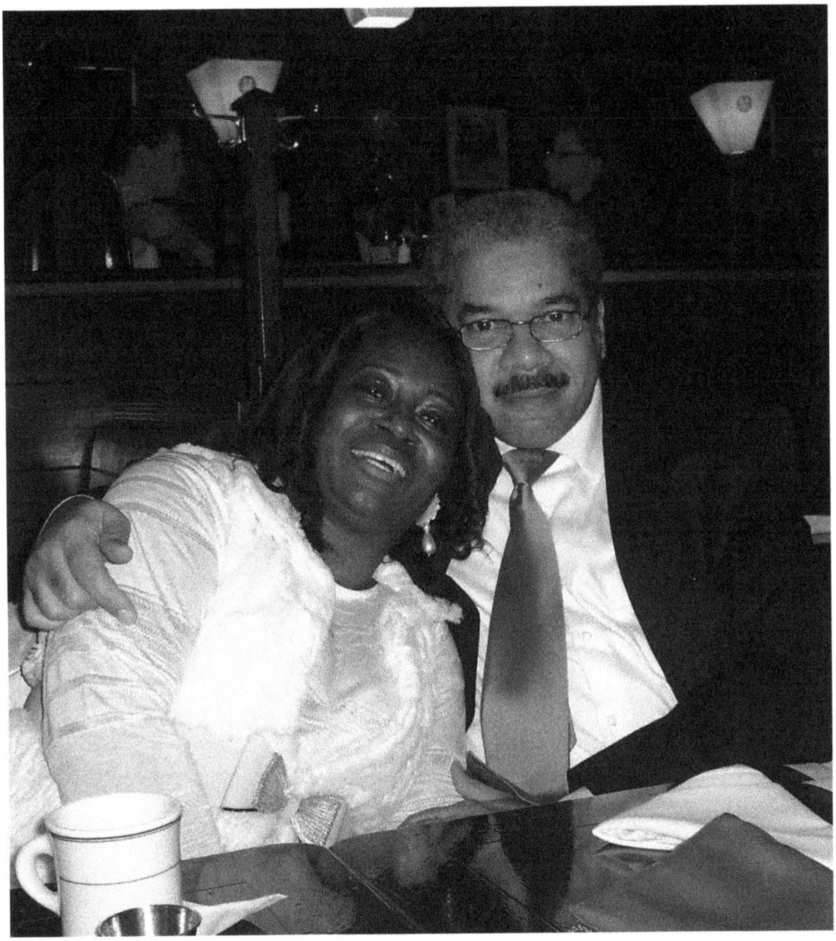

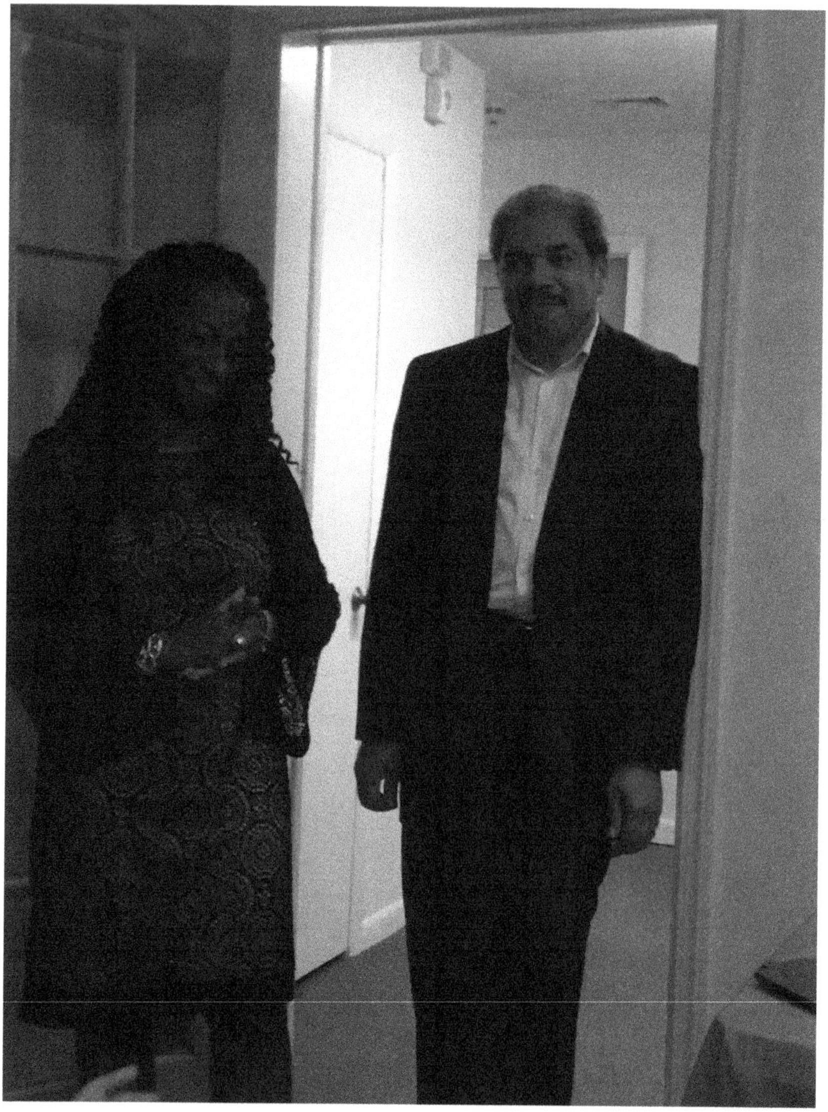

Lord Show Me Your Purpose | 131

132 | Teresa Walls

CPSIA information can be obtained
at www.ICGtesting.com
Printed in the USA
BVHW020508030419
544443BV00003B/8/P